VERTICAL GRAMMAR OF PARALLELISM
IN BIBLICAL HEBREW

ANCIENT ISRAEL AND ITS LITERATURE

General Editors:
Thomas C. Römer and Corrine L. Carvalho

Editorial Board:
Susan Ackerman
Alphonso Groenewald
Shuichi Hasegawa
Annette Schellenberg
Naomi A. Steinberg

Number 47

VERTICAL GRAMMAR OF PARALLELISM IN BIBLICAL HEBREW

David Toshio Tsumura

SBL PRESS

Atlanta

Copyright © 2023 by David Toshio Tsumura

All rights reserved. No part of this work may be reproduced or transmitted in any form or by any means, electronic or mechanical, including photocopying and recording, or by means of any information storage or retrieval system, except as may be expressly permitted by the 1976 Copyright Act or in writing from the publisher. Requests for permission should be addressed in writing to the Rights and Permissions Office, SBL Press, 825 Houston Mill Road, Atlanta, GA 30329 USA.

Library of Congress Control Number: 2023931326

Contents

Structural Patterns	vii
Abbreviations	ix

1. Definition of Parallelism 1
   1.1. What Is Parallelism? 1
   1.2. Parallelism is the device of expressing one sentence
        through two lines. 4
   1.3. Parallelism is characterized by vertical grammar,
        that is, a syntactic relation between two parallel lines. 13
   1.4. The AXB Pattern 20

2. Classification of Parallelism 25
   2.1. Formal Parallelism 26
   2.2. Semantic Parallelism 43

3. Verbal Ellipsis, Double-Duty, or Vertical Grammar 47
   3.1. Definitions 47
   3.2. Ellipsis or Double-Duty? 49
   3.3. Verbal Ellipsis or Vertical Grammar? 49

4. Vertical Grammar in Parallelism 59
   4.1. Vertical Grammar in Bicolons 59
   4.2. Vertical Grammar in Tricolons 66
   4.3. Vertical Grammar in AXX'B Tetracolons 70
   4.4. Vertical Grammar in ABXB' Tetracolons 78
   4.5. Verticality in Strophes 83

5. Syntax and Scansion in the Biblical Hebrew Poetry 85
   5.1. Enjambment in Poetic Parallelism 85
   5.2. *Kî* Clause in the Second Line 86
   5.3. *Kî* Clause in the Third Line 91

6. Janus Parallelism: Wordplay and Verticality 93

7. Verticality in Hebrew Narrative Prose 105

8. Vertical Grammar of Parallelism in Ugaritic Poetry 115

Conclusions 123

Bibliography 125
Ancient Sources Index 135
Modern Authors Index 139
Subject Index 141

Structural Patterns

AXB	the AXB pattern of literary insertion, which includes the axb pattern, the ax and b pattern, and the A//X//B pattern, as well as cases where a discourse AB is interrupted by the insertion of a discourse X and yet the narrative sequence AB is kept, such as the interruption of the Joseph story (Gen 37; 39–50) by the story of Judah and Tamar (Gen 38); the effect of such insertions is to bring a suspense to the narrative by retarding the flow
axb	the axb pattern of literary insertion where an element x is inserted between a unit ab (e.g., a construct chain) and yet the relationship of ab as a whole is kept
ax and b	the ax and b pattern of literary insertion where an element x is inserted between a unit a and b (e.g., a hendiadys) and yet the relationship of a and b as a whole is kept
A//X//B	the AXB pattern of literary insertion where a line X is inserted between a bicolon A//B and yet the unity of the bicolon is kept
a⟷b	indicates that a and b depend grammatically on each other horizontally
a↓ // b↑	indicates that a and b in two poetic lines depend on each other vertically
a–x // b–x'	indicates that a of the first line and b of the second line are grammatically dependent vertically, while x' of the second line is parallel to x of the first line, explained as a↓–x // b↑–x'
A//X//X'//B	the A-line and B-line are vertically dependent on each other, explained as A↓//X//X'//B↑; sometimes simply written as AXX'B

A↓ / B↑	the A-line and B-line are grammatically dependent vertically
X // X′	the X′-line is parallel to the X-line and is a restatement of it
a – b –c // A′ – b′	the A′ is a ballast variant of a (with an ellipsis of c′)
a – b – x // a′– X′	the X′ is a ballast variant of x (with an ellipsis of b′)

Abbreviations

General

Adv	adverb
Akk	Akkadian
Cl	clause
coref	coreferential
comp	complement
CS	compound sentence
cstr	construct
f.	feminine
M	modifier
m.	masculine
ms	masculine singular
O	object
pf	perfect
PP	prepositional phrase
qtl	verb in perfect form (suffix conjugation)
S	subject
sg.	singular
SS	simple sentence
sub	subordinate
V	verb
VE	verbal ellipsis
VG	vertical grammar
Voc	vocative
wayqtl	verb in imperfect form with a *waw* consecutive (narrative past)
weqtl	verb in perfect form (suffix conjugation) with a simple *waw* (*wə*)
XS	complex sentence

yqtl   verb in imperfect form (prefix conjugation)

Bibliographical

AB	Anchor Bible
AJBI	*Annual of the Japanese Biblical Institute*
ANES	*Ancient Near Eastern Studies*
AnOr	Analecta Orientalia
AOAT	Alter Orient und Altes Testament
ASV	American Standard Version
BA	Beiträge zur Assyriologie
BASP	*Bulletin of the American Society of Papyrologists*
BBR	Bulletin for Biblical Research
BCOTWP	Baker Commentary on the Old Testament Wisdom and Psalms
BHS	Biblia Hebraica Sttuttgartensia
Bib	*Biblica*
CAD	Gelb, Ignace J., et al. *The Assyrian Dictionary of the Oriental Institute of the University of Chicago.* 21 vols. Chicago: The Oriental Institute of the University of Chicago, 1956–2010.
CBQ	*Catholic Biblical Quarterly*
CC	Continental Commentary
COS	Hallo, William W., and K. Lawson Younger Jr., eds. *The Context of Scripture.* 4 vols. Leiden: Brill, 1997–2016.
EHLL	Khan, Geoffrey, ed. *Encyclopedia of Hebrew Language and Linguistics.* Leiden: Brill, 2013.
ESV	English Standard Version
Exeg	*Exegetica: Studies in Biblical Exegesis.* Hamura, Tokyo: Biblical Exegesis Study Group in Japan
GKC	Gesenius, Wilhelm. *Gesenius' Hebrew Grammar.* Edited by Emil Kautzsch. Translated by Arthur E. Cowley. 2nd ed. Oxford: Clarendon, 1910..
HALOT	Koehler, Ludwig, Walter Baumgartner, and Johann J. Stamm. *The Hebrew and Aramaic Lexicon of the Old Testament.* Translated and edited under the supervision of Mervyn E. J. Richardson. 2 vols. Leiden: Brill, 2001.
HdO	Handbuch der Orientalistik
HJAS	*Harvard Journal of Asiatic Studies*
HSM	Harvard Semitic Monographs

ICC	International Critical Commentary
IDB	Buttrick, George A., ed. *The Interpreter's Dictionary of the Bible*. 4 vols. New York: Abingdon, 1962.
IDBSup	Crim, Keith, ed. *Interpreter's Dictionary of the Bible: Supplementary Volume*. Nashville: Abingdon, 1976.
IOSOT	International Organization for the Study of Old Testament
JANESCU	*Journal of the Ancient Near Eastern Society of Columbia University*
JAOS	*Journal of the American Oriental Society*
JB	Jerusalem Bible
JBL	*Journal of Biblical Literature*
JNES	*Journal of Near Eastern Studies*
JNSL	*Journal of Northwest Semitic Languages*
JPS	Jewish Publication Society
JSOT	*Journal for the Study of the Old Testament*
JSOTSup	Journal for the Study of the Old Testament Supplement series
JSS	*Journal of Semitic Studies*
JTS	*Journal of Theological Studies*
KJV	King James Version
KTU	Dietrich, Manfried, Oswald Loretz, and Joaquín Sanmartín, eds. *Die keilalphabetischen Texte aus Ugarit*. Münster: Ugarit-Verlag, 2013.
LSAWS	Linguistic Studies in Ancient West Semitic
LXX	Septuagint
MT	Masoretic Text
NAC	New American Commentary
NASB	New American Standard Bible
NEB	New English Bible
NICOT	New International Commentary on the Old Testament
NIV	New International Version
NIV11	New International Version 2011
NJB	New Jerusalem Bible
NRSV	New Revised Standard Version
OBO	Orbis Biblicus et Orientalis
Orient	*Journal of the Society for the Near Eastern Studies in Japan*
OTA	Old Testament Abstracts
OTL	Old Testament Library
REB	Revised English Bible

RSV	Revised Standard Version
ScrHier	Scripta Hierosolymitana
StPohl	Studia Pohl
TOTC	Tyndale Old Testament Commentaries
UF	*Ugarit Forschungen*
VT	*Vetus Testamentum*
VTSup	Supplements to Vetus Testamentum
WBC	Word Biblical Commentary
ZAW	*Zeitschrift für die alttestamentliche Wissenschaft*
ZDMG	*Zeitschrift der Deutschen Morgenländischen Gesellschaft*

1
Definition of Parallelism

Parallelism is the poetic device of expressing "one thought through two lines." Its two basic features are repetition and correspondence of elements (i.e., sounds, affixes, words, and phrases) between two parallel lines. It is thus a linguistic and stylistic device of poetry in which two or more lines constitute a complete sentence and their elements correspond to each other semantically, grammatically, or even phonetically, with repetition and variation.

1.1. What Is Parallelism?

The phenomenon of parallelism has been long recognized in poetic texts in languages such as Chinese, Finnish, Mongolian, and Russian, as well as Hebrew, Ugaritic, and other Semitic languages. However, in the West, it was Robert Lowth who laid down the foundations of a systematic inquiry into this phenomenon in his 1778 work on the book of Isaiah. He classified Hebrew parallelism into three semantic categories: synonymous, antithetic, and synthetic.[1]

This Lowthian classification was accepted by the biblical scholars for nearly two centuries, and the initial stages of the study of the Ugaritic poetic texts after their discovery in 1929 were also influenced by this classification. However, this semantic classification has recently proved to be inadequate by the identification of stylistic categories such as the repetitive

---

1. Robert Lowth, *Isaiah: A New Translation with a Preliminary Dissertation and Notes* (London: Tegg, 1848 [orig. 1778]); also Lowth, *Lectures on the Sacred Poetry of the Hebrews*, trans. George Gregory, 3rd ed. (London: Tegg & Son, 1835), translation of *De sacra poesi hebraeorum: Praelectiones academiae Oxonii habitae* (Oxford: Clarendon, 1753).

type.² At present, it seems that Lowth's third category—synthetic parallelism—is either no longer considered to be an independent category or has been broadened to include such phenomena as the so-called expanded colon, Clines's "parallelism of greater precision," and the like.³ As a result, the term *synthetic parallelism* has become nearly meaningless.⁴

In 1966, Roman Jakobson urged a rigorous linguistic analysis of parallelism.⁵ Encouraged by his challenge, scholars such as Greenstein (1974), Collins (1978), Geller (1979), O'Connor (1980), Watson (1984), Berlin (1985) and Pardee (1988) made significant contributions to an improved understanding of Hebrew poetic parallelism by shifting the emphasis from the semantic to the grammatical component.⁶

In 1954, Peter A. Boodberg, "a master philologist in the rigorous tradition of the best early European sinologists," wrote a "penetrating prolegomena to a still missing systematic linguistic inquiry into the framework of [the Chinese poetic tradition]."⁷ Jakobson in his epoch-making 1966 article comments:

---

2. For repetitive parallelism, see the treatment in Dennis Pardee, *Ugaritic and Hebrew Poetic Parallelism: A Trial Cut*, VTSup 39 (Leiden: Brill, 1988), 6–7.

3. Adele Berlin, *The Dynamics of Biblical Parallelism* (Bloomington: Indiana University Press, 1985), 2nd ed. (Grand Rapids: Eerdmans, 2008), refers to "synthetic parallelism" only once in the index, while Wilfred G. E. Watson, *Classical Hebrew Poetry: A Guide to Its Techniques*, JSOTSSup 26 (Sheffield: JSOT Press, 1984), does not mention it at all. On the expanded colon, see Samuel E. Loewenstamm, "The Expanded Colon in Ugaritic and Biblical Verse," *JSS* 14 (1969): 176–96; Loewenstamm, "The Expanded Colon, Reconsidered," *UF* 7 (1975): 261–64. See chapter 2 on the classification of parallelism.

4. For a good summary of the history of the study of parallelism up to 1980, see Dennis Pardee, "Ugaritic and Hebrew Poetry: Parallelism," appendix 1 in Pardee, *Ugaritic and Hebrew Poetic Parallelism*, 168–92.

5. Roman Jakobson, "Grammatical Parallelism and Its Russian Facet," *Language* 42 (1966): 399–429.

6. Edward L. Greenstein, "Two Variations of Grammatical Parallelism in Canaanite Poetry and Their Psycholinguistic Background," *JANESCU* 6 (1974): 87–105; Terence Collins, *Line-Forms in Hebrew Poetry: A Grammatical Approach to the Stylistic Study of the Hebrew Prophets*, StPohl 7 (Rome: Biblical Institute Press, 1978); Stephen A. Geller, *Parallelism in Early Biblical Poetry*, HSM 20 (Missoula, MT: Scholars Press, 1979); M. O'Connor, *Hebrew Verse Structure* (Winona Lake, IN: Eisenbrauns, 1980); Watson, *Classical Hebrew Poetry*; Berlin, *The Dynamics of Biblical Parallelism*; Pardee, *Ugaritic and Hebrew Poetic Parallelism*.

7. Paul W. Kroll, review of *Selected Works of Peter A. Boodberg*, compiled by Alvin P. Cohen, *Chinese Literature: Essays, Articles, Reviews* 2 (1980): 271.

[Boodberg] has shown that a function of the second line of a couplet is "to give us the clue for the construction of the first" and to bring out the dormant primary meaning of the confronted words; he has made clear that "parallelism is not merely a stylistic device of formularistic syntactical duplication; it is intended to achieve a result reminiscent of binocular vision, the superimposition of two syntactical images in order to endow them with solidity and depth, the repetition of the pattern having the effect of binding together syntagms that appear at first rather loosely aligned."[8]

Some fifty years have passed since Jakobson claimed that "the structure of parallelism ... requires a rigorous linguistic analysis."[9] In this article, after discussing the nature of grammatical parallelism, Jakobson presented a detailed analysis of a Russian folktale. Encouraged by this challenge, a notable number of monographs were written during the late 1970s and the 1980s in the area of Hebrew and Ugaritic poetry.[10] Ever since, scholars have been making significant contributions to various aspects of the grammar and style of Hebrew poetic parallelism by shifting the "emphasis from the semantic to the syntactic component."[11] In his most recent work, Nicholas P. Lunn made a detailed theoretical analysis of word order in Biblical Hebrew poetry.[12] However, one may still feel the need for an overall rigorous *grammatical* analysis of parallelism, especially an analysis of the grammatical relation between two parallel lines.

---

8. Jakobson, "Grammatical Parallelism and Its Russian Facet," 402. For Boodberg's work, see Peter A. Boodberg, "Syntactical Metaplasia in Stereoscopic Parallelism," in *Cedules from a Berkeley Workshop on Asiatic Philology* (1954), repr. in *Selected Works of Peter A. Boodberg*, comp. Alvin P. Cohen (Berkeley: University of California Press, 1979), 184–85; see also Edward H. Schafer and Alvin P. Cohen, "Peter A. Boodberg, 1903–1972," *JAOS* 94 (1974): 1–13, which includes a bibliography of Boodberg's works.

9. Jakobson, "Grammatical Parallelism and Its Russian Facet," 400–401.

10. See the debate over Jakobson's grammatical parallelism between Ziony Zevit ("Roman Jakobson, Psycholinguistics, and Biblical Poetry," *JBL* 109 [1990]: 385–401) and Francis Landy ("In Defense of Jakobson," *JBL* 111 [1992]: 105–13). Monographs on Hebrew and Ugaritic poetry include Collins, *Line-Forms in Hebrew Poetry*; Geller, *Parallelism in Early Biblical Poetry*; O'Connor, *Hebrew Verse Structure*; James L. Kugel, *The Idea of Biblical Poetry: Parallelism and Its History* (New Haven: Yale University Press, 1981); Watson, *Classical Hebrew Poetry*; Berlin, *The Dynamics of Biblical Parallelism*; Pardee, *Ugaritic and Hebrew Poetic Parallelism*.

11. Collins, *Line-Forms in Hebrew Poetry*, 8.

12. Nicholas P. Lunn, *Word-Order Variation in Biblical Hebrew Poetry: Differentiating Pragmatics and Poetics* (Milton Keynes: Paternoster, 2006).

Jakobson in his 1966 article presented a concrete example of "a consistent linguistic analysis of pervasive parallelism" in a Russian poetic text. He noted "a typical example of a parallelism based on syntactic government" in a lament. There, a bicolon has the verb in the first line and the direct object in the second line. He stated that "not only agreement or government but also the relation between subject and predicate occasionally underlies parallel lines."[13] Thus Jakobson noted a grammatical relationship in Russian poetry in which a sentence nucleus is divided between two parallel lines. In other words, the grammatical relationship in this bicolon works *vertically*. This exact point has not been thoroughly developed in the study of Hebrew poetry.[14]

What is still needed for a rigorous linguistic analysis of parallelism is an explanation of the *vertical* grammatical relation between the parallel lines. In what follows I discuss the nature of poetic parallelism in terms of two linguistic, or syntactical, rather than stylistic, features. These have been hinted at by Boodberg and Jakobson but have not been treated concretely, especially in the study of the Hebrew poetry. I state them as follows:

(1) Parallelism is the device of expressing *one sentence through two lines*.
(2) Parallelism is characterized by *vertical grammar*, that is, a syntactic relation between two parallel lines.

1.2. Parallelism is the device of expressing one sentence through two lines.

1.2.1 Parallelism

I define parallelism semantically in the simplest way, as a poetic device expressing "one thought through two lines."[15] Here what I call two lines

---

13. Jakobson, "Grammatical Parallelism and Its Russian Facet," 428.
14. In her revised and expanded edition of *The Dynamics of Biblical Parallelism* (2008), xv–xxii, Adele Berlin briefly summarizes the history of linguistic and non-linguistic studies of parallelism and includes a three-page bibliography of materials published after 1985. There she gives two further examples, Ps 79:11 and Job 5:14, that exhibit "intricacies of parallelism." A vertical understanding of the semantic and syntactic relationships between parallel lines might allow a better explanation of such intricacies.
15. For recent discussions on the "Definitionsproblem," see Andreas Wagner, "Der Parallelismus membrorum zwischen poetischer Form und Denkfigur," in *Parallelismus*

1. Definition of Parallelism

correspond to what Boodberg describes as "two syntactic images," or two syntagms, which are superimposed and move forward together as if they were two wheels of a railway truck so that the parallel lines as a whole may carry one and unitary thought.

The metaphors of "binocular vision" (Boodberg) or "Stereoskop" (Wagner) as explanations of the function of parallelism presuppose that two lines, or cola, are the same or nearly the same in their formal, or syntactical, structures. In reality, however, two lines of parallelism exhibits a much more complicated situation.[16] My metaphor of a railway truck is similar to that of a stereoscope in the sense that both focus on one unitary image that is expressed by two separate items. However, these two superimposed lines do not always constitute an identical or similar syntactic or stylistic pattern such as a–b–c // a'–b'–c'. Less symmetrical cases such as a–b–c // c'–d'–e' also occur.

Every instance of poetry in the Hebrew language can be treated as consisting in one way or another of parallelisms in the broadest sense.[17] Contra Lunn, even lines that are semantically distinct can be clearly parallel.[18] Consider Job 13:4, where a literal translation highlights its parallelistic features:

wə'ûlām 'attem ṭōpəlê-šāqer
rōpə'ê 'ĕlîl kulləkem

However, you are the smearers of lies;
the healers of idol are you all.

The words "lies" (*šāqer*) and "idol" (*'ĕlîl*) are a word pair in the Bible (see Jer 14:14; Hab 2:18); the two construct chains "the smearers of lies" and "the healers of idol" correspond to each other not only semantically but also grammatically. No reader of Hebrew can overlook the fact that the

---

membrorum, ed. Andreas Wagner, OBO 224 (Fribourg: Academic Press; Göttingen: Vandenhoeck & Ruprecht, 2007), 1–26; and Gerald Moers, "Der Parallelismus (membrorum) als Gegenstand ägyptologischer Forschung," in Wagner, *Parallelismus membrorum*, 147–66, esp. 147–53.

16. Wagner, "Der Parallelismus membrorum," 11–13.

17. See Ernst R. Wendland, "Aspects of the Principle of 'Parallelism' in Hebrew Poetry," *JNSL* 33 (2007): 121; see also my comment below at n. 48.

18. Lunn, *Word-Order Variation*, 22 and 25 n. 60.

two lines also correspond chiastically. Such a bicolon should be treated as parallelistic.

Grammatically, however, a parallelism may be defined as a linguistic unit that constitutes one sentence through two lines. Here a *sentence* is understood as the basic thought unit. It can be either simple, compound, or complex. However, in a parallelism it is divided into two parallel lines by scansion. This explanation goes with that of Alviero Niccacci, who defines parallelism as follows: "Lines consist of parallel grammatical units, that normally constitute a complete sentence."[19]

The simple sentence here corresponds to Terence Collins's "basic sentences."[20] However, Collins's concentration on the line-form rather than on the parallel structures between two "half-lines" (i.e., cola, my "lines") leads to a denial of *paradigmatic* repetition and correspondence, as well as of the grammatical relationship between two or more parallel lines.

Similarly, James L. Kugel explains that "the basic feeling of regularity produced in Hebrew songs derives … from the recurrent sequence _____ / _____ //, an abstraction of the 'seconding' assertion 'A is so, and what's more, B.'"[21] Kugel uses the sign / to show "a slight pause" and the sign // to show "a full pause."[22]

Such an explanation might also lead us to lose sight of the grammatical relationship between two or more poetic lines. David J. A. Clines criticizes Kugel's view, explaining that Kugel " is wrong to describe the 'one sort' as a matter of 'A, and what's more, B', since that restricts the relationship of the lines to those of emphasis, repetition, seconding, and so on."[23] Clines's view, however, can be also explained as the semantic or logical interpretation of parallelism, as his own phrase, the "parallelism of greater precision," suggests.

Kugel's sign //, however, indicates the point of syntactic segmentation (the end-stopping), while / indicates the point of poetic segmentation into parallel lines.[24] In other words, a grammatical segment, that is, a sentence,

---

19. Alviero Niccacci, "Analysing Biblical Hebrew Poetry," *JSOT* 74 (1997): 89.
20. Collins, *Line-Forms in Hebrew Poetry*, 22–24.
21. Kugel, *The Idea of Biblical Poetry*, 317.
22. Kugel, *The Idea of Biblical Poetry*, 1.
23. David J. A. Clines, "The Parallelism of Greater Precision: Notes from Isaiah 40 for a Theory of Hebrew Poetry," in *Directions in Biblical Hebrew Poetry*, ed. Elaine R. Follis, JSOTSup 40 (Sheffield: JSOT Press, 1987), 95.
24. On the phenomenon of enjambment, see chapter 5.

is further segmented into poetic lines by means of scansion. Tania Notarius explains this phenomenon as "double segmentation" in poetic language.[25] She calls the two types of segmentation, grammatical segmentation and poetic segmentation. More specifically, however, I would phrase these two segmentations as segmentation by prose syntax (.) and segmentation by poetic scansion (//).[26] In light of the above, I would explain the basic form of poetic parallelism as follows:

_____ //
_____ .

Sometimes the second line constitutes an internal parallelism, as in the following:[27]

_____ //
____ // ____ .

1.2.2. Superimposition

In Hebrew poetic parallelism, two lines often constitute a compound sentence,[28] with the syntactical images of two lines being perfectly superimposed. Consider Ps 24:3:

mî yaʿăleh bəhar YHWH
ûmî yāqûm bimqôm qodšô

Who shall ascend the hill of the Lord,
and who shall stand in his holy place?

---

25. Tania Notarius, "'Double Segmentation' in Biblical Hebrew Poetry and the Poetic Cantillation System," *ZDMG* 168 (2018): 333–52.
26. On this phenomenon of double segmentation, see further below.
27. Wilfred G. E. Watson, "Internal Parallelism in Classical Hebrew Verse," *Bib* 66 (1985): 365–84; Watson, "Internal or Half-Line Parallelism in Classical Hebrew Again," *VT* 29 (1989): 44–66.
28. Collins's "Line-Type II," in which a line contains "two Basic Sentences of the same kind, in such a way that all the constituents in the first half-line are repeated in the second, though not necessarily in the same order" (Collins, *Line-Forms in Hebrew Poetry*, 23).

The syntactical structure of the first colon and that of the second are exactly the same, like most of the poetic parallelism in Chinese,[29] with the same word order of interrogative pronoun + verb + prepositional phrase:

a–b–c // a′–b′–c′.

In this *synonymous* parallelistic structure, two colons of the same syntactical image are superimposed on each other and express the meaning, "Who shall ascend the hill of Yahweh and stand in his holy place?"

On the other hand, in *antithetic* parallelism, two contrastive elements are dealt with as in Prov 15:8.

zebaḥ rəšāʿîm tôʿăbat YHWH
ûtəpillat yəšārîm rəṣônô

The sacrifice of the wicked is an abomination to the LORD,
but the prayer of the upright is his delight. (NRSV)

This is an example of superimposition of the opposite sides of the same coin, not of two contradictory thoughts.

Thus both synonymous and antithetic parallelism, the first and the second categories of Lowth's semantic classification, are two aspects of the superimposed syntactic images. With synonymous parallelism one deals with a single unitary thought from two similar angles (i.e., from the same side of the same coin); with an antithetic parallelism, the thought comes from two opposite angles (i.e., from the opposite sides of the same coin). However, in both parallelisms the two parallel lines as a whole carry a single and unitary meaning (i.e., one and the same coin).

The third Lowthian category, *synthetic* parallelism, has elicited a good deal of opposition and discussion, and nowadays the terminology is no longer used by the specialists of parallelism, as discussed in the following chapter. David Clines's "the parallelism of greater precision" is one effort to clarify some of the synthetic parallelism from the seman-

---

29. For example, in *Shih Ching*, Mao Text 234, etc. See David Jason Liu, "Parallel Structures in the Canon of Chinese Poetry: The *Shih Ching*," *Poetics Today* 4 (1983): 639–53. For *Tufu*'s Deng Gao, see David Toshio Tsumura, "Parallelism in Hebrew and Chinese Poetry," in *Philarchisophia in the Chinese and World Perspectives*, ed. Yang Shi (Beijin: Social Sciences Documentation Publishing House, forthcoming).

tic viewpoint. It constitutes what I term *hyponymous* parallelism.[30] But Clines's view is limited in that he looks at it only from the semantic side. However, the relationship between the first and the second lines can be looked at from a purely grammatical point of view, what I call vertical grammar. Of course, both hyponymous parallelism and vertical grammar deal with the same phenomenon that Dennis Pardee calls *verticality* in Biblical Hebrew parallelism, though from two different aspects of parallelism.[31]

1.2.3. Chiastic Word Order

In Ps 139:7 each line (colon) has the same syntactical image but with a chiastic word order: adverb + verb + prepositional phrase // conjunction-adverb + prepositional phrase + verb:

ʾānâ ʾēlēk mērûḥekā
wəʾānâ mippānêkā ʾebrāḥ

Where can I go from your spirit?
And where from your presence can I flee?

Here the synonymous parallelistic structure also achieves "a result reminiscent of binocular vision" and conveys the meaning, "Where shall I go away from your presence?"

A chiastic word order also appears in the antithetic parallelism in Ps 1:6:

kî-yôdēaʿ YHWH derek ṣaddîqîm
wəderek rəšāʿîm tōʾbēd

for the LORD watches over the way of the righteous,
but the way of the wicked will perish. (NRSV)

---

30. For the term *hyponymous*, see David Toshio Tsumura, "A 'Hyponymous' Word Pair, ʾrṣ and thm(t), in Hebrew and Ugaritic," *Bib* 69 (1988): 258–69. See also §2.2, below.

31. Dennis Pardee, *The Ugaritic Texts and the Origins of West-Semitic Literary Composition*, Schweich Lectures of the British Academy 2007 (Oxford: Oxford University Press, 2012), 56 n. 31.

Here, in the surface structure, particle-verb + subject + object // conjunction-subject + verb, the object of the participle of the transitive verb in the first line corresponds to the subject of the intransitive verb in the second line. In a deep grammar, both are the *patients*[32] of verbs, that is, the object of the verb "to know" (*yd*ʿ) and the subject of the verb "to perish" (*ʾbd*). Here the element "the righteous" (*ṣaddîqîm*) of line 1 is contrasted to "the wicked" (*rəšāʿîm*) of line 2. While their grammatical structures are quite distinct, the two lines simply express two different aspects of one and the same thing through parallelism. Again, the two lines are opposite sides of the same coin, each expressing the same idea from a different perspective.

1.2.4. Gapping (or Ellipsis)

Such "superimposition" of the syntactical image of two lines can also be realized even if there is a *gapping* of element in one of the parallel lines. Consider, for example, Prov 5:15:

šətēh mayim mibbôrekā
wənōzəlîm mittôk bəʾērekā

Drink waters from your own cistern,
flowing from your own well.

Here the verb is missing in the second line, and a ballast variant *mittôk bəʾērekā* (lit. "from the midst of your well") compensates for it.[33] Lunn recently explained this as a case of "dependence in gapping," in which the second line is dependent upon the first line.[34]

One might explain that the verb performs "double-duty," having a grammatical relationship both with *mayim* and with *nōzəlîm* at the same

---

32. The term *patient* refers to "the semantic role of a noun phrase denoting something that is affected or acted upon by the action of a verb" (*OED*).

33. This term *ballast variant* was first coined by Cyrus H. Gordon in *Ugaritic Textbook: Grammar, Texts in Transliteration, Cuneiform Selections, Glossary, Indices*, AnOr 38 (Rome: Pontifical Biblical Institute, 1965), 135–37. For a summary description of "ellipsis and ballast variant" in Ugaritic, see Wilfred G. E. Watson, "Ugaritic Poetry," in *Handbook of Ugaritic Studies*, ed. Wilfred G. E. Watson and Nicolas Wyatt, HdO 1.39 (Leiden: Brill, 1999), 172–73.

34. Lunn, *Word-Order Variation*, 116–17.

time.³⁵ Lunn suggests, "Drink water from your own cistern, / [drink] flowing water from your own well," supplying the "missing component," that is, the verb "drink."³⁶ However, since it is most likely that *nōzəlîm* (lit. "flowings": participle, masculine, plural) of the second line vertically modifies *mayim* (lit. "waters": noun, masculine, plural) in the first line, I take the two terms as a whole, namely, "flowing waters" (*mayim nōzəlîm*), to be the object of *šətēh*. Hence, "Drink flowing waters from your own cistern, namely, from your own well." So the entire parallelism rather constitutes a simple sentence.

We encounter something similar in Ps 47:5:

ʿālâ ʾĕlōhîm bitrûʿâ
YHWH bəqôl šôpār

God has gone up with shouts of joy,
Yahweh with the sound of a trumpet.

The lack of a verb in the second line is stylistically balanced by the ballast variant (*bəqôl šôpār*) of *bitrûʿâ* in the first line. Although Lunn explains this as an example of gapping,³⁷ this example is not like the gapping of a verb (i.e., verbal ellipsis) in prose, such as "John *ate* a fish and Meg ø a steak." Since the two subjects, God and Yahweh, in Ps 47:6 are co-referential, the second line is grammatically dependent upon the first line—and it is reasonable to think that the subject "Yahweh" and the verb ʿālâ also have a vertical grammatical relation. Therefore, the parallelism as a whole means, "God Yahweh has gone up with shouts of joy and the sound of a trumpet," *not*, "God has gone up with shouts of joy, [while] Yahweh has gone up with the sound of a trumpet." Thus here again it is evident that parallelism is the device of expressing one thought through

---

35. Alviero Niccacci, "The Biblical Hebrew Verbal System in Poetry," in *Biblical Hebrew in Its Northwest Semitic Setting: Typological and Historical Perspectives*, ed. Steven E. Fassberg and Avi Hurvitz (Jerusalem: Magnes, 2006), 258–59. For the phenomenon of double-duty elements, see Mitchell Dahood and Tadeusz Penar, "The Grammar of the Psalter," in *Psalms III, 101–150: Translated with an Introduction and Notes*, by Mitchell Dahood, AB 17A (Garden City, NY: Doubleday, 1970), 429–44. See also §3.1, below.

36. Lunn, *Word-Order Variation*, 116.

37. Lunn, *Word-Order Variation*, 19.

two lines as well as the linguistic unit that constitutes one sentence through two lines.

As for Lam 5:2, Berlin takes it as an example of verb gapping and explains that "the syntax is the same in both lines (with a gapped verb in the second line)."[38]

> *naḥălātēnû nehepkâ ləzārîm*
> *bottênû lənokrîm*

> Our land was turned over to strangers;
> Our houses to foreigners. (Berlin)

However, viewed from the perspective of vertical grammar, the paired expression *naḥălātēnû* "our land" (lit., "inheritances") and *bottênû* "our houses" is better taken as a whole (see Mic 2:2, Jer 12:7) as the subject of the verb *nehepkâ*. Hence, "Our landed property (lit., 'our land and our houses') was turned over to strangers/foreigners."[39]

Similar, though more complicated in structure, is Hab 1:2:

> ʿad-ʾānâ YHWH šiwwaʿtî wəlōʾ tišmāʿ
> ʾezʿaq ʾēlêkā ḥāmās wəlōʾ tôšîaʿ

> O Lord, how long shall I cry for help, and you will not listen?
> Or cry to you "Violence!" and you will not save? (NRSV)

Here the two lines express a single meaning: "O Yahweh, how long shall I cry to you for help, shouting 'Violence!,' and yet you will neither hear nor save?"

The above examples of "gapping" should rather be explained as cases of vertical grammatical dependence of the second line on the first. While terms such as *ellipsis* or *gapping* suggest the deletion of what was there originally, and hence that what remains is doing double-duty,[40] these

---

38. Berlin, *The Dynamics of Biblical Parallelism*, 27.

39. Cynthia L. Miller's linguistic argument concerning verbal ellipsis (gapping) in parallelism will be discussed in chapter 3, which deals with the topic of verbal ellipsis or vertical grammar in detail.

40. In his most recent study, Niccacci explains ellispsis as "the omission of a given element that is grammatically expected," which is, he holds, "particularly frequent,

examples suggest rather that grammar is working vertically between two (or more) parallel lines.

> 1.3. Parallelism is characterized by vertical grammar, that is, a syntactic relation between two parallel lines.[41]

1.3.1. Roman Jakobson

Jakobson holds that "the poetic function projects the principle of equivalence from the axis of selection into the axis of combination."[42] According to this technical definition, parallelism is the verbal structure of poetry that results when "the poet selects from the paradigmatic axis items that are equivalent and then projects them onto the syntagmatic axis in regular fashion."[43] However, poetic expression, in so far as it is a linguistic expression, is characterized by the "prose" syntax, which "is formed

---

especially in the form of a technique called 'double-duty modifier'" (Niccacci, "Biblical Hebrew Verbal System," 258–59).

41. On vertical grammar, see also David Toshio Tsumura, "Poetic Nature of the Hebrew Narrative Prose in I Samuel 2:12–17," in *Verse in Ancient Near Eastern Prose*, ed. Johannes C. de Moor and Wilfred G. E. Watson, AOAT 42 (Neukirchen-Vluyn: Neukirchener Verlag, 1993), 293; Tsumura, "Coordination Interrupted, or Literary Insertion AX&B Pattern, in the Books of Samuel," in *Literary Structure and Rhetorical Strategies in the Hebrew Bible*, ed. Lénart J. de Regt, Jan de Waard, and Jan P. Fokkelman (Assen: Van Gorcum, 1996), 119; Tsumura, "Vertical Grammar: The Grammar of Parallelism in Biblical Hebrew," in *Hamlet on a Hill: Semitic and Greek Studies Presented to Professor T. Muraoka on the Occasion of His Sixty-Fifth Birthday*, ed. Martin F. J. Baasten and Wido Th. van Peursen (Leuven: Peeters, 2003), 487–97; Tsumura, "Vertical Grammar of Parallelism in Hebrew Poetry," *JBL* 128 (2009): 167–81; Tsumura, "Parallelism," *EHLL* 3:15–19, esp. 17b–18a; and, most recently, Tsumura, "Verticality in Biblical Hebrew Parallelism," in *Advances in Biblical Hebrew Linguistics: Data, Methods, and Analyses*, ed. Adina Moshavi and Tania Notarius, LSAWS 12 (Winona Lake, IN: Eisenbrauns, 2017), 189–206: Tsumura, "Vertical Grammar of Biblical Hebrew Parallelism: The AXX'B Pattern in Tetracolons," *VT* 69 (2019): 447–59. For Ugaritic examples, see Tsumura, "Vertical Grammar of Parallelism in Ugaritic Poetry" in *"Like 'Ilu Are You Wise": Studies in Northwest Semitic Languages and Literatures in Honor of Dennis G. Pardee*, ed. H. H. Hardy II, Joseph Lam, and Eric D. Reymond (Chicago: Oriental Institute, 2022).

42. Roman Jakobson, "Linguistics and Poetics," in *Style in Language*, ed. Thomas A. Sebeok (Cambridge: MIT Press, 1960), 358.

43. Steve C. Caton, "Contributions of Roman Jakobson," *Annual Review of Anthropology* 16 (1987): 240.

along the axis of combination" and "operates via contiguity" as well as by the principle of "equivalence."[44] In prose, grammar is characterized by a horizontal or sequential (syntagmatic) combination of various linguistic elements, but in parallelistic poetry grammar works not only horizontally but also vertically.[45] Parallelism is the result of the poet's projection of the principle of contiguity from the axis of horizontal combination into the axis of vertical dependency. In other words, poetic texts are governed by vertical grammatical rules between the parallel lines as well as characterized by paradigmatic repetition and correspondence of elements (i.e., sounds, affixes, words, and phrases) between two parallel lines.

Thus Jakobson's highly technical definition, "the poetic function projects the principle of equivalence from the axis of selection into the axis of combination," fits in the nature of the "double segmentations" of poetic language, that is, syntactic segmentation (i.e., prose syntax) and poetic segmentation (i.e., scansion).[46] In poetry, the syntactic principle of equivalence works not only syntagmatically, as in prose grammar, but also paradigmatically, as in poetic grammar. I call this syntactic principle that works paradigmatically between two or more parallel poetic lines *vertical grammar*.

1.3.2. Principle of Verticality

In the Hebrew parallel structure, this phenomenon of vertical grammar can be seen in examples such as Prov 3:6:

bəkol-dərākêkā dāʿēhû   A ↓
wəhûʾ yəyaššēr ʾōrəḥôtêkā B ↑

In all your ways acknowledge him,
who makes straight your paths.

---

44. Yu-Kung Kao and Tsu-Lin Mei, "Meaning, Metaphor, and Allusion in T'ang Poetry," *HJAS* 38 (1978): 344–55.

45. Tsumura, "Poetic Nature," 293; see also Niccacci, "Analysing Biblical Hebrew Poetry," 93, which supports my view that there is a contrast between the vertical grammar of poetry and the horizontal one of prose.

46. Jakobson, "Linguistics and Poetics," 350–77. See also chapter 5 below on syntax and scansion.

Grammatically speaking, the second line depends *vertically* on the first line, while the terms of the word pair *ways* (*dərākîm*) and *paths* (*'ŏrāḥôt*), as they correspond to each other paradigmatically in a parallelism,[47] convey a sense of unity, expressing one sentence through two lines. In this example, the complex sentence ("In all your ways acknowledge him, who makes straight your paths") is divided into two parallel lines, which are in a vertical grammatical relation to each other.

Pardee in his 1988 monograph noticed occurrences of a grammatical relationship between elements of different lines as in his grammatical analysis of Prov 2:1.

```
         a      b           c
A: bənî 'im-tiqqaḥ 'ămārāy
B: ûmiṣwôtay tiṣpōn 'ittāk
         c'     d      a'
```

My son, if you accept my sayings,
Store up my commandments,

Pardee takes this as a "grammatical but not semantic parallelism" and explains that "$d = b$ grammatically."[48] Thus he recognizes that there is a grammatical relationship between element *b* in the first line and element *d* in the second. However, he did not develop this feature of poetic parallelism further.

Recently, Lunn discussed "intercolon relations," that is, "the relationships that adhere between one colon and the other(s) with which it is joined," from the aspect of modern linguistic focus theory. However, he considers only "semantic, logical, or grammatical" relationships, not phonetic ones.[49] Hence, Lunn would probably take Pardee's above example as nonparallel, based on his narrow definition of parallelism.

Thus Lunn thinks that the two colons of a bicolon are not necessarily parallel to each other because they are sometimes two grammatically independent

---

47. These two terms, both in plural form, appear as a word pair in Isa 2:3, Joel 2:7, Mic 4:2, Ps 25:4, and Prov 2:13.
48. Pardee, *Ugaritic and Hebrew Poetic Parallelism*, 94.
49. Lunn, *Word-Order Variation*, 22. See David Toshio Tsumura, review of *Word-Order Variation in Biblical Hebrew Poetry: Differentiating Pragmatics and Poetics*, by Nicholas P. Lunn, *BBR* 19 (2009): 599–600.

clauses that offer "two semantically distinct, that is non-parallel, propositions."⁵⁰ On the other hand, Ernst Wendland takes all bicola as "parallelisms," for he holds that "definite Hebrew poetry always involves parallelism—wherever two (or more) lines are viewed as a conceptual unit." He says:

> The cola concerned may not be linked by an obvious synonymous relationship, but they will characteristically be connected formally through some rhythmic accentual pattern as well as semantically in a definable way by being "two parts of a single statement."⁵¹

I would hold with Pardee that here a complex sentence is divided into two parallel clauses. The first clause ("if you accept…") in the first line is vertically dependent on the second clause ("store up…") in the second line.

To give one more example, let us look at Hab 2:8a:

```
         a         b          c
A: kî ’attâ šallôtā gôyīm rabbîm
B: yəšollûkā kol-yeter ‘ammîm
         b'          C'
```

Because you have plundered many nations,
all the remnant of the peoples shall plunder you. (ESV)

This text is a bicolon in which the two elements of the second line correspond to the two of the first line: a: "Because" (*kî*); b: "you have plundered" (*’attâ šallôtā*); c: "many nations" (*gôyīm rabbîm*) // b': "they shall plunder you" (*yəšollûkā*); C': "all the remnant of the people" (*kol-yeter ‘ammîm*). The bicolon as a whole constitutes a complex sentence in which the first line is subordinate to the second line, which is the main clause. That this is not simple prose is supported by the presence of several poetic features in this parallelism, such as the internal rhymes of ā–ā and ī–ī in the first line and –îm at the ends of both lines. Therefore, the two lines naturally have a vertical grammatical relationship.

---

50. Lunn, *Word-Order Variation*, 22 and 25 n. 60.

51. Ernst Wendland, review of *The Basics of Hebrew Poetry: Theory and Practice*, by Samuel T. S. Goh, 6 n. 5, https://tinyurl.com/SBLPress2640a. Wendland offers the examples "A: time frame—B: base event, or A: means—B: purpose."

The clearest examples of the phenomenon of vertical grammar are simple sentences divided into two or three parallel lines where at least part of the first line vertically depends on part of the second and/or third line of the parallelism. For example, Ps 18:11 constitutes a simple sentence that is divided into three parallel lines.

yāšet ḥōšek sitrô
səbîbôtāyw sukkātô
ḥeškat-mayim ʿābê šəḥāqîm

He made darkness his covering,
around him his canopy,
darkness of waters, thick clouds of the skies.

He made darkness his covering,
his canopy around him—
the dark rain clouds of the sky. (NIV)

This particular text is often divided into two parallel lines:

yāšet ḥōšek sitrô səbîbôtāyw
sukkātô ḥeškat-mayim ʿābê šəḥāqîm

He made darkness his covering around him,
his canopy thick clouds dark with water. (NRSV)

He made darkness around him his covering,
dense vapour his canopy. (REB)

Lunn also analyzes this text grammatically as a two-line parallelism: V–O–O–M // O–O.[52] However, the principle of verticality is here clearly recognizable in the three-line parallelism that should be analyzed as follows: V–O–comp / adv–comp / O. This is an example of a simple sentence divided into three parallel lines in which the second and the third line have a syntactical relation with the first by vertical grammar. Hence, the mean-

---

52. Lunn, *Word-Order Variation*, 298. Here, M stands for a clause modifier such as a prepositional phrase or an adverb.

ing of the entire parallelism is, "He made the darkness around him, that is, the darkness of waters, the thick clouds of the skies, to be his covering, that is, his canopy."

1.3.3. Vertical Parallelism

Watson notes several examples of what he calls vertical parallelism and explains as follows: "In vertically parallel lines, usually extended beyond the couplet, the correspondence between components is up and down rather than across as is the norm."[53] He cites 2 Sam 1:23 as an example of vertical parallelism:

šā'ûl wîhônātān
hanne'ĕhābîm wəhannə'îmīm
bəḥayyêhem ûbmôtām
lō' niprādû

Saul and Jonathan,
most loved and most pleasant,
in their life and in their death
were not separated.

Watson explains that schematically the first three lines can be set out as a a' / b b' / c c' instead of the more usual a b c / a' b' c' or the like.[54]

However, Watson's vertical parallelism is stylistic and has nothing to do with a vertical grammatical relationship between the lines. In fact, he ignores the fourth line, where the key element of the sentence, the predicate (*lō' niprādû*), appears and does not discuss the relationship between it and the subjects in the first two lines. In the same way, Gzella's "vertikaler *Parallelismus*" is not concerned with a vertical grammatical relation between two parallel lines.[55]

---

53. Watson, *Classical Hebrew Poetry*, 158.
54. Watson, *Classical Hebrew Poetry*, 158.
55. See Holger Gzella, "Parallelismus und Asymmetrie in ugaritischen Texten," in Wagner, *Parallelismus membrorum*, 133–38.

1.3.4. Vertical Grammar

Unlike the vertical parallelism above, vertical grammar is concerned with the grammatical relation between lines, often a simple sentence being divided into two or three lines vertically. For example, vertical grammar is recognizable in the poetic structure of Mic 7:3b:

haśśar
        šōʿēl
// *wəhaššōpēṭ baššillûm*

The prince
        asks,
also the judge, for a bribe. (NASB)

While RSV and ESV translate "the prince and the judge ask for a bribe," NIV unjustifiably supplies "gifts" and "accepts" and translates: "the ruler demands gifts, the judge accepts bribes." However, the prepositional phrase *baššillûm* vertically depends on the participle *šōʿēl* in the first line; hence there is no need to supply "gifts" in the first line. Watson calls this pattern a "synonymous-sequential parallelism" and explains the pair "the prince" and "the judge" as parallel, and "asks" and "for a payment" as "continuous."[56] I would rather explain it as x–a // x′–b, in which x (*haśśar*) and x′ (*haššōpēṭ*) are parallel (x//x′) and a (*šōʿēl*) and b (*baššillûm*) are in a vertical grammatical relation (a–b).[57]

The vertical grammatical relationship can be most clearly illustrated by such examples as Ps 18:41, which has the pattern a–x // b–x′.

yəšawwəʾû wəʾên môšiaʿ
ʿal-YHWH wəlōʾ ʿānām

They cried for help, but there was none to save,
to the LORD, but he did not answer them.

---

56. Watson, *Classical Hebrew Poetry*, 157.
57. For the a–x // b–x′ type, see Tsumura, "Vertical Grammar: The Grammar of Parallelism in Biblical Hebrew," 490–92.

Here "to the LORD" (b) in the second line vertically modifies "They cried for help" (a) in the first line, while the clause "but he did not answer them" (x') in the second line is a further specification of "but there was none to save" (x). The poetic structure can be explained as

wəʾên môšîaʿ (x)
yəšawwəʾû (a) // ʿal-YHWH (b)
wəlōʾ ʿānām (x')

The verb phrase yəšawwəʾû (a) // ʿal-YHWH (b) holds a grammatical relationship with the two parallel elements (x // x') *as a whole*. It should be noted that this is not an example of ellipsis or gapping, for if one supplies "they cried" in the second line, one needs also to supply "to the LORD" in the first line, as follows:

yəšawwəʾû [ʿal-YHWH] wəʾên môšîaʿ
[yəšawwəʾû] ʿal-YHWH wəlōʾ ʿānām

Such an underlying syntactical structure would be too prosaic for a poetic parallelism.

1.4. The AXB Pattern

In the AXB pattern, X is inserted between the AB complex and yet A and B hold their unity while X holds its grammatical or semantic relationship with AB *as a whole* rather than with A and B *at the same time*.[58] When I referred to this pattern as literary insertion in my 1981 Jerusalem paper, I focused on the literary phenomenon of insertion (X) between the normally unseparated items (AB) of phrases such as construct chains and hendiadyses.[59] Such insertion causes a literary breakup and has an effect of retardation (suspension) of the narrative flow in order to give the audience a sense of tension and expectation. Here, on the other hand, I focus

---

58. See David Toshio Tsumura, "Literary Insertion (AXB Pattern) in Biblical Hebrew," *VT* 33 (1983): 468–82; "Literary Insertion, AXB Pattern, in Hebrew and Ugaritic: A Problem of Adjacency and Dependency in Poetic Parallelism," *UF* 18 (1986): 351–61; "Coordination Interrupted, or Literary Insertion AX&B Pattern," 117–32.

59. David Toshio Tsumura, "Literary Insertion (AXB) Pattern in Biblical Hebrew," in *Proceedings of the Eighth World Congress of Jewish Studies,1981, Division A: The Period of the Bible* (Jerusalem: World Union of Jewish Studies, 1982), 1–6.

on the grammatical relation between the separated items, that is, A and B. Even if these items appear in separate parallel lines as A // B, A and B still hold their semantic or grammatical relationship to each other vertically.

1.4.1. Composite Phrase

One of the typical examples of the vertical grammatical relation between two parallel lines is the breakup of a construct chain (a of b) into two parallel lines, as in Isa 64:10b (MT 9b):

ṣîyôn midbār hāyātâ
yərûšālayim šəmāmâ

Zion has become a wilderness,
Jerusalem, a desolation.

In this text, the construct chain *midbar šəmāmâ* "desolate wilderness" (a of b; lit., "wilderness of desolation"; Jer 12:10, Joel 2:3, 3:19 [MT 4:19]) is split up into two parts, one in the first line, the other in the second (a // b). In other words, these two words are vertically related grammatically.[60] Hence the meaning is, "Zion Jerusalem has become a desolate wilderness," *not* "Zion has become a wilderness, while Jerusalem [has become] a desolation."

Psalm 18:8 (MT 9) offers another example:

ʿālâ ʿāšān bəʾappô
wəʾēš mippîw tōʾkal
geḥālîm bāʿărû mimmennû

Smoke went up from his nostrils,
and devouring fire from his mouth;
glowing coals flamed forth from him. (NRSV)

Here the construct chain *gaḥălê ʾēš* "coals of fire" (v. 12) is broken up by the parallelism into *ʾēš* // *geḥālîm* ("fire" // "coals").

---

60. Ezra Z. Melamed, "Break-Up of Stereotype Phrases as an Artistic Device in Biblical Poetry," in *Studies in the Bible*, ed. Chaim Rabin, ScrHier 8 (Jerusalem: Magnes, 1961), 136–37. See most recently, Simeon Chavel, "Biblical 'Alternation' and Its Poetics," in Hardy, Lam, and Reymond, *"Like ʾIlu Are You Wise,"* 179–203.

Psalm 24:6 also presents a case of the breakup of a composite phrase (a of b) into two parallel lines (a // b), as I explain elsewhere.[61]

zeh dôr dōrəšāw
məbaqšê pānêkā yaʿăqōb

This is the generation, those who seek him,
those who seek your face, of Jacob.

Here, most probably, the genitive construction *dôr yaʿăqōb* ("the generation of Jacob": a of b) is broken up into two parts in the parallelism: *dôr* // *yaʿăqōb*.

zeh dôr yaʿăqōb (a of b)
dōrəšāw (x)
məbaqšê pānêkā (x')

This is the generation of Jacob,
those who seek him
those who seek your face.

X (*dōrəšāw* [x] // *məbaqšê pānêkā* [x']) is inserted between a and b, thus constituting the AXB pattern: a–x // x'–b.

1.4.2. Compound Phrase

Similarly, a compound phrase (a and b) can be divided into two elements, one in the first line and the other in the second line (a // b), yet these two behave as if they are one unit. Such a vertical grammatical relationship is typical of parallelistic structure in poetry, as in Ps 2:4:

yôšēb baššāmayim yiśḥāq
ʾădônāy yilʿag lāmô

He who sits in the heavens laughs;
the Lord scoffs at them.

---

61. Tsumura, "Vertical Grammar: The Grammar of Parallelism in Biblical Hebrew," 491–92.

This can be interpreted as

yôšēb baššāmayim yiśḥāq //
                              lāmô
ʾădônāy   yilʿag

He who sits in the heavens laughs //
                                     at them
the Lord scoffs

Here what appears to be the verbal compound "laugh and scoff" (a and b) is split up into two parts, one in the first line, the other in the second (a // b). Hence the phrase "at them" (*lāmô*) modifies the entire verbal phrase. The meaning of the parallelism as a whole is: "He who sits in the heavens, that is, the Lord, laughs and scoffs at them."[62]

Consider also Ps 22:2:

ʾĕlōhay ʾeqrāʾ yômām wəlōʾ taʿăneh
wəlaylâ wəlōʾ-dûmîyâ lî

O my God, I cry by day, but you do not answer,
and by night, but I find no rest. (ESV)

Here the composite word (*or* phrase) pair "by day and by night" (a and b) is split up into two parts, one (a) in the first line, the other (b) in the second line. Yet the parallel words, a // b, as a whole modifies one and the same verb ("I cry").

Thus "the two halves of the verse are interdependent to such an extent that they frequently form together a single syntactical structure."[63] In other words, the grammar of poetic parallelism is characterized not only

---

62. One can take the compound "laugh and scoff" as a verbal hendiadys that is split up into two parallel lines not only stylistically but also grammatically. Here, too, my basic theses—parallelism is the device of expressing *one sentence through two lines* and parallelism is characterized by *vertical* grammar—are applicable.

63. Melamed, "Break-Up of Stereotype Phrases," 152. It should be noted that, while Melamed emphasizes the literary phenomenon of break-up of a syntactical unit into parallel lines, I focus on the *vertical* grammatical relationship of the two elements.

by the usual horizontal grammar but also by vertical grammar[64] in which the elements of parallel lines have a grammatical relationship with each other vertically. Parallelism is not simply a stylistic device of poetry but is a linguistic phenomenon that has its own grammar.

---

64. See Tsumura, "Vertical Grammar: The Grammar of Parallelism in Biblical Hebrew," 487–97; David Toshio Tsumura, "Vertical Grammar—The Grammar of Parallelism," in *The First Book of Samuel*, NICOT (Grand Rapids: Eerdmans, 2007), 55–59; see also Takamitsu Muraoka, "Between Linguistics and Philology," *ANES* 41 (2004): 87–88.

2
Classification of Parallelism

The classification of parallelism remains a contentious issue, and scholars continue to suggest various new categories or patterns. Traditionally, Robert Lowth's classification has been standard among biblical scholars. It uses three *semantic* categories: synonymous, antithetical, and synthetical parallelism.[1] However, the definition of synthetical parallelism is vague, and there has been a tendency to use it as a catch-all category for anything other than synonymous or antithetical parallelism.

The discovery of Ugaritic poetic texts beginning in 1929 shed light on the *stylistic* aspects of poetic parallelism in Biblical Hebrew, the basic feature of which is repetition. For example, the so-called expanded colon, a type of repetitive parallelism, has been noted as a characteristic in both Ugaritic and Hebrew poetic texts. In addition, parallel word pairs common to both languages have been identified as the corollary of parallelistic analysis of Hebrew and Ugaritic poetry.[2] Although these word pairs are not limited to poetic texts, poetic parallelism certainly encouraged two words to become fixed as a pair as a stylistic feature.

However, since the latter half of the 1960s, formal aspects of poetic parallelism have been noted on the *grammatical* levels, especially since Roman Jakobson's promotion of a "rigorous" linguistic analysis of poetic parallelism, as noted above.

In this chapter I will first classify parallelism from the formal aspect, which includes phonetic parallelism, then from the semantic aspect. I will

---

1. See chapter 1.
2. See Mitchell Dahood, "Ugaritic-Hebrew Parallel Pairs," in *Ras Shamra Parallels: The Texts from Ugarit and the Hebrew Bible*, ed. Loren R. Fisher and Stan Rummel, 3 vols. (Rome: Pontifical Biblical Institute, 1972), 1:1–33; Yitshak Avishur, *Stylistic Studies of Word-Pairs in Biblical and Ancient Semitic Literatures*, AOAT 210 (Neukirchen-Vluyn: Neukirchener Verlag, 1984).

note especially the meaning relationship between two (or more) parallel lines (colons).

The basic unit of parallelism naturally consists of two parallel lines (an A line and a B line), and this unit is usually called a *bicolon* (A//B). This cohesive unit of two parallel lines may not only develop into a three- to five-line parallelism but also may be reduced to a single line, a monocolon.[3] Here one may notice that the term *line* is used as a basic unit of parallelism, as in the phrase "parallel lines"; technically, the line is same as the colon, which generally consists of three or four words.

In the case of a three-line parallelism (a tricolon), the third line may simply be a repetition of the first line, normally with some sort of variation, as in A//B//A'. Or it may be a repetition, with variation, of the second line: A//B//B'. In special cases, the first line is repeated, with variation, in the second line, then followed by the original second line of a bicolon, as in A//A'//B. Such a pattern has been called an expanded colon. A bicolon may be interrupted by the insertion of a distinct "middle" line (X), thus creating an A//X//B pattern.[4] This pattern is distinct from both A//B//A' and from the expanded colon A//A'//B. Sometimes a bicolon (x//y) is inserted between another bicolon (A//B), creating A//x//y//B.[5] Other patterns of four- or five-line parallelism, that is, tetracolon or pentacolon, also occur. In the following, I present concrete examples that illustrate these various patterns of parallelism.

2.1. Formal Parallelism

The formal parallelisms are classified first according to the relation between the parallel lines and then according to the phonetic correspondence.

---

3. For the various groupings of cola, see Watson, *Classical Hebrew Poetry*, 177–87. The term *monocolon* is used here for "isolated colon," which is "always a sentence" (Stanislav Segert, *A Basic Grammar of the Ugaritic Language* [Berkeley: University of California Press, 1984], 108); see also Segert, "Parallelism in Ugaritic Poetry," *JAOS* 103 [1983]: 297 [295–306]; Watson, *Classical Hebrew Poetry*, 12; cf. "orphan lines" in Jakobson, "Grammatical Parallelism and Its Russian Facet," 429.

4. For the first article that dealt with this "literary" phenomenon of Hebrew Bible, see Tsumura, "Literary Insertion (AXB) Pattern in Biblical Hebrew," 1–6.

5. David Toshio Tsumura, "'Inserted Bicolon,' the AXYB Pattern, in Amos I 5 and Psalm IX 7," *VT* 38 (1988): 234–36.

2.1.1. Parallel lines

2.1.1.1. Monocolon

A single colon (monocolon) may appear at a crucial point within a poem, such as at the beginning, at the midpoint, or at the final, conclusive point.

Monocolon at Beginning

> Ps 18:1
> *'erḥāməkā YHWH ḥizqî*
> I love you, O Lord, my strength. (ESV)

> Ps 139:1
> *YHWH ḥăqartanî wattēdāʿ*
> O Lord, you have searched me and known me!

In these examples, with three words in each, there is no way to divide the line into two; the line is a monocolon. At the beginning of these psalms, the psalmist expresses his close and intimate relationship by these short and simple phrases.

> Ps 23:1
> *YHWH rōʿî lōʾ ʾeḥsār*
> The Lord is my shepherd; I shall not want.

In Ps 23:1, the line is most probably a monocolon, though one can theoretically divide it into two short lines, with two words in each line.

Monocolon in Middle

> Ps 92:7-9 (MT 8-10)
> ⁸ *biprōaḥ rəšāʿîm kəmô ʿēśeb*
> *wayyāṣîṣû kol-pōʿălê ʾāwen*
> *ləhiššāmədām ʿădê-ʿad*
> ⁹ *wəʾattâ mārôm ləʿōlām YHWH*
> ¹⁰ *kî hinnēh ʾōyəbeykā YHWH*
> *kî-hinnēh ʾōyəbeykā yōʾbēdû*
> *yitpārədû kol-pōʿălê ʾāwen*

> ⁷ that though the wicked sprout like grass
> and all evildoers flourish,
> they are doomed to destruction forever;
> ⁸ but you, O Lord, are on high forever.
> ⁹ For behold, your enemies, O Lord,
> for behold, your enemies shall perish;
> all evildoers shall be scattered. (ESV)

Here the monocolon of verse 8 is sandwiched between two tricolons (vv. 7 and 9) and expresses the Lord's sovereignty with confidence. Verse 10 constitutes an expanded colon of the A//A'//B pattern.[6]

> Song 5:6
> *pātaḥtî 'ănî lədôdî*
> *wədôdî ḥāmaq ʿābār*
> *napšî yāṣəʾâ bədabbərô*
> *biqqaštîhû wəlōʾ məṣāʾtîhû*
> *qərāʾtîw wəlōʾ ʿānānî*
>
> I opened to my beloved,
> but my beloved had turned and gone.
> My soul failed me when he spoke.
> I sought him, but found him not;
> I called him, but he gave no answer. (ESV)

This verse has five lines. No one doubts that the last two lines, the fourth and the fifth, constitute a bicolon. As for the first three lines, although Watson takes them as a tricolon, these lines can be divided as a bicolon and a monocolon. Thus the monocolon is sandwiched between two bicolons and expresses the maiden's deep feeling toward her beloved.

Monocolon at End

> Ps 150:6
> *kōl hannəšāmâ təhallēl yāh*
> *haləlû-yāh*

---

6. See p. 30, below.

Let everything that has breath praise the LORD!
Praise the LORD!

The final phrase, "Praise the LORD!" (*halǝlû-yāh*), is a formula and constitutes a literary frame with the identical phrase that opens verse 1. The first part of verse 6 is thus to be taken as a monocolon.

2.1.1.2. Tricolon

Frequently a tricolon follows an A//B//A′ or A//B//B′ pattern.

A//B//A′

Watson lists Gen 27:39 as an example of a tricolon with a chiastic structure:

hinnēh mišmannê hāʾāreṣ
yihyeh môšābekā
ûmiṭṭal haššāmayim mēʿāl

    A   See, from the fat of the earth
    B   shall your dwelling be,
    A′ and from the dew of heaven above.[7]

A//B//B′

Watson cites Hos 9:16a for the A//B//B′ pattern:

hukkâ ʾeprayim
šoršām yābēš
pǝrî bǝlî-yaʿăśûn

    A   Stricken is Ephraim:
    B   their root withered,
    B′ no fruit shall it bear.[8]

In these examples one of the first two lines (A // B) is repeated with a variation.

---

7. Watson lists more than fifty examples (*Classical Hebrew Poetry*, 182).
8. Translation from Watson, *Classical Hebrew Poetry*, 181.

A//A'//B: Expanded Colon

A bicolon (A//B) is often expanded into a tricolon. The expanded line may be a repetition of the A-line with variation, thus A//A'//B, like the expanded colons in the following examples:[9]

Ps 92:9
kî hinnēh ʾōyəbeykā YHWH
kî-hinnēh ʾōyəbeykā yōʾbēdû
yitpārədû kol-pōʿălê ʾāwen

A For behold, your enemies, O Lord,
A' for behold, your enemies shall perish;
B all evildoers shall be scattered. (ESV)

Prov 31:4
ʾal lamlākîm ləmôʾēl
ʾal lamlākîm šətô-yāyin
ûlrôzənîm ʾê [qere] šēkār

A (Let there be) not for kings, O Lemuel,
A' (let there be) not for kings (any) drinking of wine,
B yea, for rulers (let there be) no (drinking of) strong drink,[10]

A//X//B[11]

A tricolon with an A//X//B pattern is rare. In this pattern, an X-line, a line completely different from its context either semantically or grammatically, is inserted between the two lines of a bicolon A//B. Note that the third example below (2 Sam 1:21) follows an A//X//and B pattern.

Gen 49:8
yəhûdâ ʾattâ yôdûkā ʾaḥeykā

---

9. Loewenstamm, "Expanded Colon," 176–96; see Greenstein, "Two Variations of Grammatical Parallelism," 87–105.

10. See David Toshio Tsumura, "The Vetitive Particle אֵ and the Poetic Structure of Proverb 31:4," *AJBI* 4 (1978): 28.

11. On the principle of the "literary insertion" (AXB pattern), see §1.4 above.

yādəkā bəʿōrep ʾōyəbeykā
yištaḥăwû ləkā bənê ʾābîkā

Judah, your brothers shall praise you;
your hand shall be on the neck of your enemies;
your father's sons shall bow down before you.

1 Sam 2:2
ʾên-qādôš kaYHWH
kî ʾên biltekā
wəʾên ṣûr kēʾlōhênû

There is none holy like the Lord:
for there is none besides you;
there is no rock like our God.

2 Sam 1:21
hārê baggilbōaʿ
ʾal-ṭal wəʾal-māṭār ʿălêkem
ûśədê tərûmōt

O mountains in Gilboa,
let there be no[12] dew and no rain upon you!
and fields of the heights.

Other examples are 1 Sam 2:3a, 13; 3:1; 28:19; 2 Sam 12:9; Pss 5:7; 6:11; 9:15; 22:2; 40:7; 49:8, 14; 51:16, 18, 21; 86:12.[13]

2.1.1.3. Tetracolon

Parallelism may also consist of four parallel lines. Such a tetracolon is distinct from the pattern of two contiguous bicolons or that of a monocolon followed by a tricolon. However, it is often hard to identify a genuine tetracolon. For example, Ps 46:6 is usually translated as:

---

12. The negative particle *ʾal* is repeated.
13. Tsumura, "Literary Insertion (AXB Pattern)," 479–82; Tsumura, "Coordination Interrupted," 124–27.

The nations rage, the kingdoms totter;
he utters his voice, the earth melts. (ESV)

However, there has been a persistent view that the verse should be analyzed as a tetracolon, thus:

hāmû gôyīm
māṭû mamlākôt
nātan bəqôlô
tāmûg ʾāreṣ

The nations rage,
the kingdoms totter;
he utters his voice,
the earth melts.

On the other hand, Prov 23:15–16 has been traditionally analyzed as a succession of two bicolons:

¹⁵ *bənî ʾim-ḥākam libbekā*
yiśmaḥ libbî gam-ʾānî
¹⁶ *wətaʿlōznâ kilyôtāy*
bədabbēr śəpāteykā mêšārîm

My son, if your heart is wise,
my heart also will be glad.
My inmost being will exult
when your lips speak what is right.

However, for reasons discussed below, the text as a whole should be analyzed as a tetracolon.

Song 5:1a
bāʾtî ləgannî ʾăḥōtî kallâ
ʾārîtî môrî ʿim-bəśāmî
ʾākaltî yaʿrî ʿim-dibšî
šātîtî yênî ʿim-ḥălābî

I came to my garden, my sister, my bride,

> I gathered my myrrh with my spice,
> I ate my honeycomb with my honey,
> I drank my wine with my milk.

The issue with Song 5:1a is whether one should take these four lines as constituting a tetracolon or a monocolon followed by a tricolon. A monocolon may occur at a key position, as noted above, especially at the first line (e.g., Pss 18:1; 23:1; 139:1. Here the MT scansion, V M [Voc] // V O M // V O M // V O M, seems to suggest this possibility.[14] The differences between the first line and the following three lines are certainly noticeable both grammatically and semantically. Nevertheless, the repetition of the same grammatical form, *qal* perfect first common singular (*bāʾtî, ʾārîtî, ʾākaltî, šātîtî*), with an assonance of /tî/, suggests that the four lines are to be treated as a whole. One should note also that assonance of [î] occurs throughout the entire verse, appearing three times in every line, twelve times total. With these phonetic repetitions among four lines, it seems preferable to take this verse as a four-line parallelism. Watson also takes this verse as an example of an ABB'B" quatrain, that is, a tetracolon.[15]

The [Voc] at the end of the first line rather supports the idea that the action "I came" in the first line is succeeded by "I gathered," hence "I came and gathered." Such a [Voc] typically appears in the case of an expanded colon,[16] an original bicolon a b // a' b' expanded to a [Voc] // a b // a' b', as was seen above in Ps 92:9.

Taking Song 5:1 as a tetracolon with the assonance of [î], J. Cheryl Exum notes that "the man emphasizes his claim to the garden both by the sequence 'I come ... I pluck ... I eat ... I drink' and by the eightfold repetition of 'my': 'I come to *my* garden, *my* sister bride, I gather *my* myrrh with *my* spice, I eat *my* honeycomb with *my* honey, I drink *my* wine with *my* milk.'"[17] Thus, it is reasonable to take the four lines as a whole as constituting a parallelistic structure.

---

14. M stands for "clause modifier" (PP or Adv). According to Lunn, the sign / designates "a major pause in a poetic line," while on the other hand the sign // denotes "the relationship of poetic parallelism." See Lunn, *Word-Order Variation*, xxi–xxii; for his grammatical analysis of Song 5:1–16, see 362–63.

15. Wilfred G. E. Watson, "Verse Patterns in the Song of Songs," *JNSL* 21 (1995): 115.

16. Loewenstamm, "The Expanded Colon, Reconsidered," 261–64.

17. J. Cheryl Exum, *Song of Songs: A Commentary*, OTL (Louisville: Westminster John Knox, 2005), 153, 181.

A//B//A'//B': Alternating Parallelism[18]

Ps 38:3
'ên-mətōm bibśārî
mippənê zaʿmekā
'ên-šālôm baʿăṣāmay
mippənê ḥaṭṭā'tî

There is no soundness in my flesh
because of thy indignation;
there is no health in my bones
because of my sin.[19]

Ps 106:24-25
wayyim'ăsû bə'ereṣ ḥemdâ
lō'-he'ĕmînû lidbālô
wayyērāgnû bə'ohŏlêhem
lō' šāməʿû bəqôl YHWH

And they despised the pleasant land,
and they did not have faith in his promise,
and they murmured in their tents,
and they did not obey the voice of Yahweh.

Isa 34:6
ḥereb laYHWH
mālə'â dām
huddašnâ mēḥēleb

---

18. John T. Willis, "Alternating (ABA'B') Parallelism in the Old Testament Psalms and Prophetic Literature," in *Directions in Biblical Hebrew Poetry*, ed. Elaine R. Follis, JSOTSup 40 (Sheffield: JSOT Press, 1987), 49-76. Chavel's recent essay on the poetic phenomenon of alternation deals with the following passages as examples of "alternation as a rhetorical figure": Isa 62:8-9; Deut 32:42; Isa 34:6a; Ps 113:5-6; Jer 34:9; and Exod 25:7 (Chavel, "Biblical 'Aternation' and Its Poetics"). However, the first two examples (Isa 62:9; Deut 32:42) are better explained as cases of vertical grammar (VG); see chapter 3 below.

19. Translation from Willis, "Alternating (ABA'B') Parallelism," 53.

2. Classification of Parallelism

middam kārîm wəʿattûdîm
mēḥēleb kilyôt ʾêlîm

[The LORD has a sword];
it is sated with blood,
it is gorged with fat,
with the blood of lambs and goats,
with the fat of the kidneys of rams.[20]

A//B//B'//A'

In the A//B//B'//A' pattern, the second half (B'//A') is a mirror image of the first half (A//B), as in Prov 23:15–16:[21]

[15] *bənî ʾim-ḥākam libbekā*
yiśmaḥ libbî gam-ʾānî
[16] *wətaʿlōznâ kilyôtāy*
bədabbēr śəpāteykā mêšārîm

My son, if your heart is wise,
my heart also will be glad.
My inmost being will exult
when your lips speak what is right.

A//X//B//X'[22]

    Song 5:12
    ʿênāyw kəyônîm   A↓
    ʿal-ʾăpîqê māyim   X
    rōḥăṣôt beḥālāb   B↑
    yōšəbôt ʿal-millēʾt   X'

His eyes are like doves
beside streams of water,

---

20. Translation from Willis, "Alternating (ABA'B') Parallelism," 66. Chavel ("Biblical 'Aternation' and Its Poetics," §4) cites this example as having an alternating structure.
21. See Berlin, *The Dynamics of Biblical Parallelism*, 87.
22. for X//A//X'//B, see §3.3, below.

bathed in milk,
sitting beside a full pool. (ESV)

This passage is extremely difficult, and it has been said that "there is no certain interpretation of this verse." Roland E. Murphy and S. Dean McBride Jr., after citing various suggestions, make the conjectural insertion of "teeth," which they think "makes the metaphor of the milk bath and fullness more intelligible; the reference then would be to the white teeth set in firm gums."[23] Othmar Keel, on the other hand, keeps the MT as it is and interprets the subject of "bathed in milk" as the doves. According to him, "the milk baths indicate that the poet is talking about white doves."[24] He translates the third line as "[(like doves)] bathed in milk."[25]

Here it is most likely that the phrase ʿal-ʾăpîqê māyim ("beside streams of water") in the second line is restated in the fourth line with a participle in yōšəbôt ʿal-millēʾt ("sitting beside a full pool"). Moreover, the third line depends on the first grammatically, since ʿênāyw ("his eyes") and rōḥăṣôt ("washing") are both feminine plural. Hence, "His eyes are washing in milk." As Richard Hess notes, the colored part of his eyes, that is, the irises and pupils, is here set in contrast to the "field of white within the eye."[26] Similarly, Exum says that the doves suggest "the pupil and iris surrounded by the milky whiteness of the eye."[27] If this interpretation is correct, we have a nuclear sentence "his eyes are washing in milk," into which is inserted the simile "like doves [f. pl.] beside streams of water." So, we have the following:

His eyes, like doves beside streams of water, are washing in milk.

---

23. Roland E. Murphy and S. Dean McBride Jr., *The Song of Songs: A Commentary on the Book of Canticles or the Song of Songs*, Hermeneia (Minneapolis: Fortress, 1990), 172.

24. Othmar Keel, *The Song of Songs*, CC (Minneapolis: Fortress, 1994), 199.

25. Keel, *The Song of Songs*, 196. Duane A. Garrett comments: "חלב, 'milk,' simply gives the metaphor ["like doves"] in a more exaggerated form since milk implies richness. There is obviously no reason that a bird would actually bathe in milk" (Duane A. Garrett and Paul R. House, *Song of Songs and Lamentations*, WBC 23B [Dallas: Word, 2004], 220).

26. Richard S. Hess, *Song of Songs*, BCOTWP (Grand Rapids: Baker Academic, 2005), 182.

27. Exum, *Song of Songs*, 204-5.

The imagery of milk baths certainly fits eyes better than doves.

As for the subject of the feminine plural participle *yōšabôt* ("sitting") in the fourth line, the other feminine plural noun, "doves," is the most likely candidate grammatically as well as semantically, since "eyes" do not "dwell" or "sit."

While Hess thinks that in lines 2 and 4 the imagery shifts to water, "a possible allusion to the tears,"[28] I prefer to see the same imagery for all four lines, that is, the "freshness" of the eyes and the doves. Hence, I take lines 2 and 4 as describing the situation of doves in line 1. Doves by the waterside would certainly give a fresh and youthful impression.[29]

Therefore, in this four-line parallelism, the first (A) and third (B) lines are vertically dependent on each other (A↓/B↑), while the fourth (X') is a restatement of the second (X) with some additional information (X//X'). Thus, a grammatical understanding of parallelism helps to clarify the metaphor. The four lines of the parallelism—

His eyes are, like doves
beside streams of water,
washing in milk,
dwelling beside a full pool

—can be reduced to the following two parallel ideas:

His eyes are washing in milk,
like doves beside streams of water, dwelling beside a full pool.

A parallelistic structure similar to the A//X//B//X' pattern can be recognized elsewhere in both Hebrew and Ugaritic poetry, such as Jer 4:23 (a–b//X//B'//X') and *KTU* 1.14.i.26-27, 33-35 (a–b–x//B'–x').[30]

---

28. Hess, *Song of Songs*, 183.
29. Marvin H. Pope, *Song of Songs: A New Translation with Introduction and Commentary*, AB 7C (Garden City, NY: Doubleday, 1977), notes: "The bright eyes of the lover, the dark pupils encircled by milky white eyeballs, remind the poet of doves bathing in pellucid streams" (538). See also Robert Alter, *The Art of Biblical Poetry* (New York: Basic Books, 1985), 197.
30. See Tsumura, "Vertical Grammar of Parallelism in Hebrew Poetry," 178-79.

A//x//y//B → A//X//X'//B[31]

Sometimes a bicolon (x//y) is inserted between another bicolon (A//B). Such an inserted bicolon, the A//x//y//B pattern, is attested in the following examples

> Amos 1:5
> wəšābartî bərîaḥ dammeśeq
> wəhikrattî yôšēb mibbiqʻat-ʼāwen
> wətômēk šēbeṭ mibbêt ʻeden
> wəgālû ʻam ʼărām qîrâ
>
> I will break down the gate of Damascus;
> I will cut off the enthroned one from the Valley of Awen,
> namely, the one who holds the scepter from Beth Eden;
> the people of Aram will go into exile to Kir.[32]
>
> Ps 9:6 (MT 7)
> hāʼôyēb tammû
> ḥŏrābôt lāneṣaḥ
> wəʻārîm nātaštā
> ʼābad zikrām hēmmâ
>
> The enemy are destroyed—
> as ruins forever
> cities you have uprooted—
> even the memory of them has perished.[33]

Other examples are 2 Sam 7:22 and Ps 89:36–37 (MT 37–38),[34] as well as 2 Sam 3:33b–34, Job 12:24–25, Ps 17:1, Isa 35:4, Hos 11:10, Mic 2:4, and Hab 3:13b.[35] This pattern is not same as the envelope construction.[36] While

---

31. See below, §4.3.
32. Tsumura, "'Inserted Bicolon,' the AXYB Pattern," 234–35.
33. Tsumura, "'Inserted Bicolon,' the AXYB Pattern," 235–36.
34. Tsumura, "Vertical Grammar of Biblical Hebrew Parallelism," 447–59. See chapter 4 below.
35. Tsumura, "Coordination Interrupted," 127–28.
36. See, for example, Francis I. Andersen and David Noel Freedman, *Hosea: A*

in the envelope construction (AXX'A') AX and X'A' are mirror images, in the AxyB pattern AB is interrupted by the insertion of a bicolon (x//y) that is often totally different from AB.

2.1.1.4. Pentacolon

For an example of a pentacolon, we have Hab 1:8:

> wəqallû minnəmērîm sûsāyw
> wəḥaddû mizzəʾēbê ʿereb
> ûpāšû pārāšāyw
> ûpārāšāyw mērāḥôq yābōʾû
> yāʿūpû kənešer ḥāš leʾěkôl

> Their horses are swifter than leopards,
> more fierce than the evening wolves;
> their steeds charge.
> Their horsemen come from afar;
> they fly like an eagle swift to devour.[37]

The first two colons of this verse are a perfect bicolon with the ballast variant (*mizzəʾēbê ʿereb*) corresponding to the shorter phrase *minnəmērîm*. It describes the swiftness of the Babylonians' horses (*sûsāyw*). On the other hand, the last two colons constitute another bicolon, describing a sequence of activities of the Babylonian horsemen (*pārāšāyw*): "they come and swoop like an eagle." The image of devouring prey fits the activities of the horsemen rather than the horses, for horses normally do not devour. Thus the pentacolon constitutes the pattern bicolon (II) – monocolon (I) – bicolon (II), in which a monocolon is inserted between two bicolons, thus constituting an A//X//B pattern.[38] Note that the unbalanced, short, colon

---

New Translation with Introduction and Commentary, AB 24 (Garden City, NY: Doubleday, 1980), 301.

37. David Toshio Tsumura, "Polysemy and Parallelism in Hab 1,8–9," *ZAW* 120 (2008): 202.

38. See Tsumura, "Vertical Grammar: The Grammar of Parallelism in Biblical Hebrew," 487. There are various types of inserted colons. One might note the examples of insertion of a bicolon (xy) between two colons (A and B), namely, an inserted bicolon (AxyB), in Amos 1:5 and Ps 9:6, as well as examples of an inserted tricolon

"their steeds charge" (*ûpāšû pārāšāyw*) in the middle might be intentional, as a short colon often appears in the center of tricolons of a pivotal pattern.[39]

2.1.2. Phonetic Parallelism

Poetic parallelism can be analyzed not only semantically but also grammatically and phonetically. In this regard, Dennis Pardee's 1988 analysis of Prov 2 and Anat I is a significant contribution to advancing our understanding of the nature of parallelism, by noting in detail both grammatical and phonetic parallelism.[40]

> Prov 2:1
> *bənî 'im-tiqqaḥ 'ămāray*
> *ûmiṣwôtay tiṣpōn 'ittāk*
>
> My son, if you accept my sayings,
> store up my commandments.

Pardee analyzes the phonetic parallelism as follows:[41]

> Like vowel in accented syllable: -*qa*- , -*rā*- / -*ta*- , -*tā*-
> Like vowel in final syllable: -*aḥ*- , -*āy*- / -*ay*- , -*āk*-

Psalm 2:6 shows an a b c pattern in the first line and a d D' pattern in the second:

(AxyzB) in Ugaritic texts such as *KTU* 1.3.iv.48–53, v.40–43; cf. 1.4.i.12–18, iv.52–57. See Tsumura, "'Inserted Bicolon,' the AXYB Pattern," 234–36.

39. Tsumura, "Polysemy and Parallelism in Hab 1,8–9," 199. See Mitchell Dahood, "A New Metrical Pattern in Biblical Poetry," *CBQ* 29 (1967): 574; Wilfred G. E. Watson, "The Pivot Pattern in Hebrew, Ugaritic, and Akkadian Poetry," *ZAW* 88 (1976): 249; Watson, "Verse-Patterns in Ugaritic, Akkadian and Hebrew Poetry," *UF* 7 (1975): 489–91.

40. Pardee, *Ugaritic and Hebrew Poetic Parallelism*. In the same volume, in the appendix "Types and Distributions of Parallelism in Ugaritic and Hebrew Poetry" (193–201; originally 1982), Pardee calls attention to the importance of the study of types of parallelism, "especially in the relatively new field of grammatical parallelism and in the relatively neglected field of phonetic parallelism."

41. Pardee, *Ugaritic and Hebrew Poetic Parallelism*, 134.

waʾănî nāsaktî malkî
ʿal-ṣiyôn har-qodšî

I have installed my king
on Zion, my holy mountain.

Although some may not consider these two lines parallel, I consider them as constituting a parallelism with a rhyme *malkî*//*qodšî* (*-î* // *-î*), that is, a phonetic parallelism. Note the repetitive use (alliteration) of /i:/ in the bicolon as well as that of /ʿal/ – /har/ (assonance).

Song 5:1a
bāʾtî ləgannî ʾăḥōtî kallâ
ʾārîtî môrî ʿim-bəśāmî
ʾākaltî yaʿrî ʿim-dibšî
šātîtî yênî ʿim-ḥălābî

I came to my garden, my sister, my bride,
I gathered my myrrh with my spice,
I ate my honeycomb with my honey,
I drank my wine with my milk.

In the four lines of Song 5:1a, one can easily recognize the repetition of the sound /i:/, which shows that this tetracolon constitutes a phonetic parallelism.

Song 5:2
ʾănî yəšēnâ wəlibbî ʿēr
qôl dôdî dôpēq

I was sleeping, and my heart was awake;
there was a sound! My beloved was knocking.

These two lines can be interpreted as follows: "When I was sleeping, though my heart was awake, there was a sound; my beloved was knocking." The first line constitutes an "inner parallelism"[42] and provides the setting for the subordinate clause stating when a "sound" came to her. It

---

42. Watson, "Verse Patterns in the Song of Songs," 112.

should be noted that this bicolon is replete with assonances such as *î – î //
î, ē – ē // ē* in the two lines and *ô – ô – ô* in the second line, as well as alliterations of *q* and *d* in the second line, right after *qôl* "voice." Even though the two lines seem to Lunn to be "nonparallelistic" semantically,[43] they are certainly parallel to each other phonetically.

The next lines are:

*pitḥî-lî ʾăḥōtî raʿyātî
yônātî tammātî*

Open to me, my sister, my love,
my dove, my perfect one,

These two lines exhibit a simple parallelism, an elaborate repetition of an element (vocative) of the first line in the second line, V M [Voc] // [Voc]. This example illustrates that the basic feature of poetry is "repetition with variation" of the same element, here [Voc]: a–b // b′. For examples illustrating the vertical grammar of parallelism, see §3.3.2, below. Note that every word in this parallelism end with the same syllable: an assonance of /ī/.

The last two lines constitute a typical bicolon:

*šerrōʾšî nimlāʾ-ṭāl
qəwuṣṣôtay rəsîsê lāylâ*

for my head is drenched with dew,
my locks with the drops of the night.

This example can be classified as an example of verbal ellipsis (VE), where the verbal form is gapped in the second line. If one takes the basic sentence structure of parallelism in this verse as a compound sentence (CS) where the verb of the first line is repeated in the second line, one must supply the verb "are drenched" in the second line.

However, there is another way of explaining this parallelism, that is, taking the entire sentence as a simple sentence (SS). I would take this bicolon *vertical grammatically* (VG). The bicolon as a whole has only one verb

---

43. On Lunn's position, see p. 15, above.

"is drenched" and constitutes a simple sentence where the two lines are "superimposed" on each other:[44]

> For my head with dew
> is drenched,
> my locks with the drops of the night.

The entire parallelism means, "For my head, that is, my locks, are drenched with dew, namely, the drops of the night."[45]

2.2. Semantic Parallelism

Ever since the discovery of Ugaritic poetic texts, the Lowthian semantic classification of parallelism into synonymous, antithetical, and synthetical has been reevaluated. Unlike the third category, the first two categories are well accepted by scholars.

2.2.1. Synonymous Parallelism

Synonymous and antithetic parallelism are both aspects of the superimposed syntactic images, as noted above (§1.2.2). With synonymous parallelism one looks at a thought from two similar angles (i.e., from the same side of the same coin), while with antithetic parallelism one looks from two opposite angles (i.e., from the opposite sides of the same coin). However, in both types of parallelism the two parallel lines as a whole carry a single, unitary meaning (i.e., one and the same coin).

While word pairs are basic constituents of synonymous or antithetical parallelism, parallelism itself often encouraged the production of word pairs. For a semantic discussion of any word pair, it is not enough to analyze the meaning of each word etymologically. The meaning relation between such paired words should be investigated thoroughly and placed adequately in their context of parallelism.

---

44. For the syntactic aspect of parallelism, see Tsumura, "Vertical Grammar of Parallelism in Hebrew Poetry," 167–81, esp. 169–74.
45. For a detailed discussion concerning the difference between the verbal ellipsis (VE) and the vertical grammar (VG), see Chapter III.

2.2.2. Hyponymous Parallelism

Traditionally, the meaning relation of a word pair has been treated either as synonymy or antonymy. However, for some word pairs, such as "hand" and "right hand," the meaning relation is hyponymy.[46] This is sometimes explained as inclusion: what term A refers to *includes* what term B refers to.[47] But the term *hyponymy* is preferable to *inclusion*, for it is "a relation of sense which holds between lexical items" rather than a relation of "reference," that is, "entities which are named by lexical items."[48] The inclusion thus entails hyponymy, but hyponymy can be used also for a relationship between terms that have no reference.

Our term hyponym therefore means that the sense [A] of the more general term A (e.g., fruit) includes the sense [B] of the more specific term B (e.g., apple), and hence what A refers to includes what B refers to, and B is hyponymous to A. For example, *ymyn* "right hand" is hyponymous to *yd* "hand," since what the term *ymn* refers to is normally a part of what the term *yd* refers to. Thus an analysis of meaning relations in terms of meaning inclusion (= hyponym) is extremely profitable for the semantic discussions of word pairs, for, set in the context of poetic parallelism, the two terms seem to acquire a closer association to each other than in an ordinary prose context.

The hyponymous relation between paired words such as fruit–apple has been noted in Hebrew also by Berlin, who explains the relation as a device of *particularizing*.[49] Berlin's "particularizing" parallelism (e.g., Ps 29:5) and Clines's "parallelism of greater precision"[50] (e.g., Isa 40:16) are hyponymous parallelisms in our terms, as distinguished from synonymous parallelisms.

---

46. For the term *hyponymous*, see Tsumura, "A 'Hyponymous' Word Pair," 258–69.

47. Charles R. Taber ("Semantics," *IDBSup*, 803–4) lists four types of "conceptual relationships between the sense of different forms": synonymy and similarity; inclusion; antonymy; and polar opposition.

48. Cf. John Lyons, *Semantics*, 2 vols. (Cambridge: Cambridge University Press, 1977); Lyons, *Introduction to Theoretical Linguistics* (Cambridge: Cambridge University Press, 1968), 453–55.

49. Adele Berlin, "Parallel Word Pairs: A Linguistic Explanation," *UF* 15 (1983): 11; Berlin, *The Dynamics of Biblical Parallelism*, ch. 4.

50. See Clines, "The Parallelism of Greater Precision," 77–100, esp. 96 n. 2.

Ps 29:5
qôl YHWH šōbēr ʾărāzîm
wayšabbēr YHWH ʾet-ʾarzê hallǝbānôn

The voice of the Lord breaks cedars;
the Lord smashes the cedars of Lebanon.[51]

Isa 40:16
ûlbānôn ʾên dê bāʿēr
wǝḥayyātô ʾên dê ʿôlâ

And Lebanon is not enough for burning,
and its animals not enough for a burnt offering.

The term hyponymous is usually used in semantics to describe the relationship between two words. Berlin describes the meaning relation between two words such as *yd* ("hand") and *ymyn* ("right hand") as "a term // [i.e., parallel to a] subordinate, that is, *yd* is the more general term and *ymyn* is a subcategory of it," a relationship sometimes called "hyponymous."[52] Here I would like to use hyponymous also for the relation between two parallel lines. In other words, the first line presents a theme or item in a general sense, while in the parallel line it is focused by a detailed description with greater precision. In such a case, the meaning relation between the two parallel lines is not so much synonymous as hyponymous, since what the first line refers to includes what the second line refers to.

The third Lowthian category, synthetic parallelism, has generated significant opposition and discussion, and today the terminology is no longer used by specialists in parallelism, as noted above (§1.2.2). David Clines's parallelism of greater precision has been described by Dennis Pardee as the "most perceptive statement" on the rhetorical function of parallelism for clarifying aspects of synthetic parallelism from the semantic viewpoint.[53] However, Clines's view is limited in that he looks only at the semantic side.

---

51. Adele Berlin, "Shared Rhetorical Features in Biblical and Sumerian Literature," *JANES* 10 (1978): 37.

52. Berlin, *The Dynamics of Biblical Parallelism*, 15.

53. See Pardee, *The Ugaritic Texts*, 56 n. 31, 92. Pardee noted that I did not make reference to Clines's work in my 2009 article. The reason is that my paper was about

One can also look at the relationship between the first and second lines as a purely grammatical phenomenon, that is, vertical grammar. Of course, both hyponymous parallelism and vertical grammar deal with the same phenomenon that Pardee calls *verticality* in Biblical Hebrew parallelism, though from two different aspects of parallelism.[54]

---

grammar, while Clines's important observation on the nature of parallelism was about semantics.

54. Pardee, *The Ugaritic Texts*, 56 n. 31, 92.

3
Verbal Ellipsis, Double-Duty, or Vertical Grammar

While in prose grammar dependency operates between elements horizontally, in the grammar of poetic parallelism it sometimes operates between the elements of parallel lines, that is, vertically. In this chapter I examine the possibility of establishing linguistic rules for the vertical grammar of poetic parallelism in Biblical Hebrew.

In a parallelistic structure, a bicolon has a pattern such as a–b (–c) // a′–b′ (–c′), often with variation. We see this in every language that takes parallelism as the basic poetic expression, such as Hebrew, Ugaritic, Akkadian, and Chinese. In most cases, elements are in a grammatical relationship with other elements in the same line, that is, *horizontally*. However, in rarer cases, there is also a grammatical relation between the elements of different lines, that is, *vertically*. The normal bicolon has the pattern a–b // a′–b′, where a has a relationship with b and a′ with b′. However, sometimes a bicolon follows the pattern of $a\downarrow$–x // $b\uparrow$–x′, where a and b, although in different lines, are related grammatically to each other, while x′ is simply a restatement of x. In other words, the a–b relationship is a vertical grammatical dependence, while the x–x′ relationship is a paradigmatic repetition.

Before we investigate the vertical grammatical relation over parallel lines, we should clarify some terminology that has been used in the discussions of poetic parallelism in Biblical Hebrew.

3.1. Definitions

3.1.1. Horizontal Grammar

In an ordinary parallelism with the pattern a–b // a′–b′, the elements of each line have grammatical relationships only with elements of the same

line, that is, horizontally, so a and b have a grammatical relationship (⟷),
as do a′ and b′ (⟷).

3.1.2. Vertical Grammar

In some rarer cases, an element in the first line holds a grammatical relationship with an element in the second line *vertically*. An example would be the following pattern a–x // b–x′ (a–b as vertical grammar):

a↓–x
b↑–x′

In this case, a and b have a vertical grammatical relationship, while x′ in the second line is simply a restatement of x in the first line.

3.1.3. Ellipsis

Ellipsis originally developed as a term in stylistics, *gapping* in grammar. However, the idea of gapping comes from prose grammar, which is horizontal. Ellipsis is a structure in which a line a–b–c is parallel to a line a′–b′, where it appears that c′ in the deep structure has been gapped.

a–b–c // a′–b′–(c′) [c′ as ellipsis] ← deep grammar

3.1.4. Double-Duty

In a double-duty structure a line a–b–c is likewise parallel to a′–b′, but in this case c, which has no corresponding element in the second line, is understood as doing double-duty; in other words, c has a grammatical relation to a′–b′ and to a–b *at the same time*.

a–b–c // a′–b′ [c as double-duty] ← surface grammar

The difference between ellipsis and double-duty is that ellipsis is concerned with the deep structure and double-duty with the surface structure. The term double-duty has been used in the context of style.[1] Grammatically,

---

1. For the relationship between double-duty and gapping, see §1.2.4, above.

the relationships between c and a–b as well as c and a′–b′ are grammatical. So, that between c and a′–b′ is a vertical grammar.

[a ⟷ b] ⟷ c ↓
[a′ ⟷ b′] ↑

3.2. Ellipsis or Double-Duty?

In order to understand various possible ways of analyzing Hebrew poetic parallelism, let us examine Ps 8:4:

    a   b   c
mâ-ʾĕnôš kî-tizkərennû
ûben-ʾādām kî tipqədennû
      B′   c′

The underlying structure of Ps 8:4 is usually understood as *mâ-ʾĕnôš //* (*mâ*) *ben-ʾādām*: "What is a human being… // and (what is) a son of man…?," with the particle *mâ* ellipsized in the second line.

Alternatively, *mâ* in the first line might be explained as double-duty, that is, as modifying *ʾĕnôš* and *ben-ʾādām* at the same time.[2] In other words, in this explanation the grammatical relationship between *mâ* (a) and *ʾĕnôš* (b) is horizontal (a⟷b), while that of *mâ* (a) and *ben-ʾādām* (B′) is vertical (a↓ / ↑B′). The translation would thus be: "What is a human being… // and a son of man…?," thus a⟷b / ↑B′.

The third way of explanation is that the particle *mâ* (a) modifies the composite phrase "a human being, namely, a son of man" as a whole (b, namely, B′). In this case it is *ʾĕnôš* and *ben-ʾādām* that hold a vertical relationship (b↓ / ↑B′) of apposition between the two parallel lines: "What is a human being, namely, a son of man…?"

3.3. Verbal Ellipsis or Vertical Grammar?

Among various possibilities, the most crucial topic is whether a particular example is that of a verbal ellipsis (VE)[3] or that of a vertical grammar (VG). There are some difficulties in distinguishing these two phenomena.

---

2. See Tsumura, "Vertical Grammar of Parallelism in Hebrew Poetry," 172.
3. For the phenomenon of verbal ellipsis in Biblical Hebrew poetry, see Cyn-

Hab 3:3a [VE] a–b–c // a′–b′
    a   b   c
'ĕlôah mittêmān yābô'
wəqādôš mēhar-pā'rān
     a′   B′

The bicolon of Hab 3:3a is normally understood as a compound sentence with verbal ellipsis,[4] or gapping, where the underlying sentence structure is a compound sentence and the verb is gapped in the second line. Thus it is translated:

God (a) came (c) from Teman (b);
the Holy One (a′) [came (c′)] from Mount Paran (B′).

Stylistically, the gapped element c′ (*yābô'*) is compensated in the second line by a ballast variant *mēhar-pā'rān* (B′) of its corresponding element, *mittêmān*, in the first line. Thus the pattern can be analyzed as a–b–c // a′-B′-(c′).

An alternative explanation is that the verb, element c (V), is doing double-duty, taking both *'ĕlôah* (a) and *qādôš* (a′) as its subject at the same time. Grammatically, the element c (V) governs a horizontally and a′ vertically. Since a and a′ are semantically coreferential, grammatically a and a′ as a whole (a+a′) seem to have a relation with the verb (c) in the first line. In this case, the two terms (a and a′) are in apposition, vertical grammatically. In this explanation the meaning of the bicolon is:

God (a), namely, the Holy One (a′), came (c)
from Teman (b), specifically from Mount Paran (B′).

---

thia L. Miller, "A Linguistic Approach to Ellipsis in Biblical Poetry (Or, What to Do When Exegesis of What Is There Depends on What Isn't)," *BBR* 13 (2003): 251–70; Miller, "Ellipsis Involving Negation in Biblical Poetry," in *Seeking Out the Wisdom of the Ancients: Essays Offered to Honor Michael V. Fox*, ed. Ronald L. Troxel, Kelvin G. Friebel and Dennis R. Magary (Winona Lake, IN: Eisenbrauns, 2005), 37–52.

4. Other examples of vertical ellipsis are Ps 105:20 (VG in Tsumura, "Vertical Grammar of Parallelism in Hebrew Poetry"); Jer 4:23 (VG in Tsumura, "Vertical Grammar of Parallelism in Hebrew Poetry"); Pss 2:8b; 18:14; Prov 26:14; Isa 1:27. The phenomenon of verbal ellipsis has been studied in detail by Cynthia Miller.

3. Verbal Ellipsis, Double-Duty, or Vertical Grammar

3.3.1. Verbal Ellipsis

In an earlier article I explained Ps 18:14 and 105:20 as examples of vertical grammar (VG), namely, a syntactic relation between two parallel lines, but now I believe they are more likely to be examples of verbal ellipsis (VE), for both are easily analyzed as a pattern of a–b–c // (a')–b'–c'.

> Ps 18:14
>   a   b   c
> *wayyišlaḥ ḥiṣṣāyw waypîṣēm*
> *ûbərāqîm rāb wayhummēm*
>   (a') B'   c'

This bicolon is usually analyzed as an example of VE: a–b–c // (a')–B'–c':

> And he sent out his arrows and scattered them;
> he flashed forth lightnings and routed them. (ESV)

The phrase "he flashed forth" is supplied as a gapped element. A more literal translation would be:

> And he sent out (a) his arrows (b) and scattered them (c);
> and (a': he sent out) great lightnings (B') and routed them (c').

Another case is Ps 105:20 [VE]:

>   a   b   c
> *šālaḥ melek wayyattîrēhû*
> *mōšēl ʿammîm waypattəḥēhû*
>   B'   c'

Similarly, though ESV (also JPS, NIV, REB) takes "the ruler of the peoples" as preposed before the conjunction *waw*, translating "The king sent and released him; / the ruler of the peoples set him free," this verse is better understood as an example of VE: a–b–c // (a')–B'–c'. Thus a woodenly literal translation for this VE would be:

> The king (b) sent (a) and released him (c);
> the ruler of the peoples (B') (a': sent) and set him free (c');

Job 40:5 is also an instance of verbal ellipsis, here with the verbal element b′ ellipsized.

```
    a          b        c
'aḥat dibbartî wəlōʾ ʾeʿĕneh
ûštayim      wəlōʾ ʾôsîp
    a'                  c'
```

Once (a) I have spoken (b), and I will not answer (c);
Twice (a′), but I will proceed no further (c′).

In Jer 4:23 the prepositional phrase *ʾel-haššāmayim* (B′) has a vertical grammatical relation with the verb *rāʾîtî* (a) in the first line.[5]

rāʾîtî (a) *ʾet-hāʾāreṣ* (b)
wəhinnēh-tōhû wābōhû (x)
wəʾel-haššāmayim (B′)
wəʾên ʾôrām (x′)

I looked at the earth,
and it was desolate and empty;
and to the heavens,
and their light was gone.

The parallelistic structure is the same as that in the previous examples: a–b–x // B′–x′. The meaning is, "I look at the earth and the heavens, and the earth was desolate and empty, while the heavens were without the light."[6]

3.3.2. Vertical Grammar

It is difficult to think that the next examples show verbal ellipsis; vertical grammar is a better explanation.

---

5. For this verse, see David Toshio Tsumura, *Creation and Destruction: A Reappraisal of the Chaoskampf Theory in the Old Testament* (Winona Lake, IN: Eisenbrauns, 2005), 28–32.

6. The same pattern, a–b–x // B′–x′, may be attested also in such Ugaritic texts as *KTU* 1.14.i.26–27 (VG) and 33–35 (VE).

Ps 18:41 a↓–x // b↑–x′
    a↓   x
yəšawwəʿû wəʾên-môšîʿ
ʿal-YHWH wəlōʾ ʿānām
    b↑   x′

This text has been translated literally in KJV as:

> They cried, but there was none to save them:
> even unto the LORD, but he answered them not. (KJV)

However, most of the modern versions supply "they cried" in the second line:

> They cried for help, but there was none to save;
> they cried to the LORD, but he did not answer them. (RSV, ESV;
> also NRSV, REB, JPS)

Here "to the LORD" (b) in the second line vertically modifies "They cried for help" (a) in the first line, while the clause "but he did not answer them" (x′) in the second line is a further specification of "but there was none to save" (x). It should be noted that this is *not* an example of ellipsis or gapping, for if one supplies "they cried" in the second line, one needs also to supply "to the Lord" in the first line.[7]

yəšawwəʿû (ʿal-YHWH) wəʾên-môšîʿ
(yəšawwəʿû) ʿal-YHWH wəlōʾ ʿānām

Such an underlying syntactical structure would be too prosaic for poetic parallelism.

A good English translation, though it destroys the Hebrew surface structure, might be a–b // x–x′:

> Though they cried for help (a) to the LORD (b),
> there was none to save them (x), nor did he answer them (x′).

A similar example is Hab 3:16a, which has the structure a↓–x // b↑–x′:

---

7. See below on Mic 7:3.

```
    a↓         x
šāmaʿtî wattirgaz biṭnî
ləqôl ṣālălû śəpātay
    b↑         x′
```

This bicolon has a more complicated structure than the previous ones. It has been taken as having the structure of a–b–c // d–b′–c′. It may be translated literally as:

I listened, and my body trembled;
to the sound my lips quivered.

Here the phrase "to the sound" is usually understood as horizontally governed by the verb "quivered." For example, the ESV translates:

I hear, and my body trembles;
my lips quiver at the sound.

However, it is more likely that it should be analyzed as a↓–x // b↑–x′, where the element "to the sound" (b) in the second line is the complement of "I listened" (a) in the first line vertically, while the other elements "my body trembled" (x) and "my lips quivered" (x′) constitute a kind of merismus with regard to the physical response to the sound, the former referring to an internal response and the latter to an external one.[8] Hence, the entire bicolon may be translated as a–b // x–x′:

(When) I listened (a) to the sound (b),
my body trembled (x) and my lips quivered (x′).

Let us look at another case, Mic 7:3b, which was already dealt with in chapter 1. This half-verse has a structure x–a↓ // x′–b↑:

haśśar šōʾēl
wəhaššōpēṭ baššillûm

---

8. The term merismus refers to the literary practice of putting side by side two opposite terms to expressing a totality of everything between the two extremes. These can be binary opposed terms such as *internal* and *external*, gradual opposite terms such as *big* and *small*, or polar opposite terms such as *heavens* and *earth*.

The prince (x) asks (a),
and the judge (x'), for a bribe (b).

This text also is usually analyzed as a–b–(c) // a'–(b')–c', with the object ellipsized in the first line and the verb in the second line:

The prince (a) asks (b) ([c]);
and the judge (a') ([b']) for a bribe (c').

Some translations are:

the ruler demands gifts,
the judge accepts bribes. (NIV)

The magistrate makes demands,
And the judge [judges] for a fee. (JPS)

However, a mixture of forward and backward gappings seems unnatural.[9] It seems better to analyze it as x–a↓ // x'–b↑, in which "for a bribe" (b) is *vertically* dependent on "asks" (a).

The prince (x) asks (a)
and the judge (x') for a bribe (b).

Hence, the meaning of the entire bicolon is: "The prince and the judge ask for a bribe." This translation is exactly that of the RSV, though the English translation does destroy the Hebrew parallelistic structure:

x–x' // a–b: the prince (x) and the judge (x') ask (a) for a bribe (b).

Chavel deals with passages such as Isa 62:8–9 and Deut 32:42 as examples of "alternation as a rhetorical figure."[10] I prefer to explain these as cases of vertical grammar. Consider, for example, Isa 62:9:

---

9. See also Ps 18:41 (above). For forward and backward ellipsis, see Miller, "A Linguistic Approach," 263.

10. Chavel, "Biblical 'Alternation' and Its Poetics." Some of his examples are classified in the alternating parallelism ABA'B' pattern (above).

kî məʾaspāyw yōʾkəlūhû   *wəhiləlû ʾet-YHWH*
ûm(ə)qabbəṣāyw yištūhû   *bəḥaṣrôt qodšî*

those who gather it shall eat it   and they shall praise Yahweh
and those who collect it shall drink in my holy courts. (Chavel)

Chavel explains this text as follows:

> Just as the heads of the two lines (vv. 9aα and 9bα), מְאַסְפָּיו יֹאכְלֻהוּ and וּמְקַבְּצָיו יִשְׁתֻּהוּ, directly correlate with each other to suggest an identical relationship of work and enjoyment, so too in the two tails (vv. 9aβ and 9bβ), וְהִלְלוּ אֶת־יְהוָה bears an intimate relationship with בְּחַצְרוֹת קָדְשִׁי, that of action defined by space: they shall praise Yahweh in his holy courts.[11]

He explains the phenomenon from both rhetorical and semantic aspects as a "blending of lines, the vertical reading," and a "sequential reading." I would explain the same phenomenon from grammatical aspect. This passage exhibits the x–a↓ // x′–b↑ pattern, where b modifies a vertical grammatically, while x and x′ are a typical bicolon in which two colons are perfectly parallel to each other. An alternative solution might be to analyze the verse as a tetracolon:[12]

məʾaspāyw yōʾkəlūhû	X
wəhiləlû ʾet-YHWH	A↓
ûm(ə)qabbəṣāyw yištūhû	X′
bəḥaṣrôt qodšî	B↑

In the alternation of four lines, the first set x – x′ constitutes a perfect parallelism:

> those who gather it shall eat it,
> and those who collect it shall drink.

The entire bicolon is a merismatic parallelism. On the other hand, the set a–b forms a simple sentence with a *vertical* grammar:

> and they shall praise the Lord

---

11. Chavel, "Biblical 'Alternation' and Its Poetics," 183.
12. See my most recent article, Tsumura, "Vertical Grammar of Biblical Hebrew Parallelism," 447–59. See also chapter 4, below.

3. Verbal Ellipsis, Double-Duty, or Vertical Grammar

in my holy courts.

Another instructive example is found in Deut 32:42:

'aškîr ḥiṣṣay middām   wəḥarbî tō'kal bāśār
middām ḥālāl wəšibyâ   mērō'š par'ôt 'ôyēb

I drench my arrows with blood   and my blade consumes flesh
with the blood of corpse and captive from the wild heads of the enemy.

Here Chavel similarly explains that "reading the verse in alternation rather than sequentially resolves it into two coherent, consistent statements: Yahweh drenches his arrows with the blood of corpse and captive, and his blade consumes … the flesh by severing heads from their respective bodies."[13] He explains the alternating structure as giving rhetorical vividness and highlights the dynamic sense of the poetry. However, his appreciation of the parallelism is rhetorical and semantic, not grammatical.

I would explain this example as the pattern of x – a // x' – b or as a tetracolon, the pattern of which is X // A // X' // B.

'aškîr ḥiṣṣay middām   X
wəḥarbî tō'kal bāśār   A↓
middām ḥālāl wəšibyâ   X'
mērō'š par'ôt 'ôyēb   B↑

In either pattern X and X' is a typical parallelism as a bicolon:

I drench my arrows with blood   X
with the blood of corpse and captive X'

That is, X' is a restatement of X with a verbal ellipsis and a ballast variant. On the other hand, A and B constitute a vertical grammar; that is, the lines A and B depend on each other vertically.

and my blade consumes flesh   A↓
from the wild heads of the enemy.   B↑

---

13. Chavel, "Biblical 'Alternation' and Its Poetics," 185.

4
Vertical Grammar in Parallelism

It was Dennis Pardee who used the term *verticality* for my examples of vertical grammar, and I totally agree with him concerning the designation for the cases of vertical grammar (VG) discussed here. However, verticality is a wider concept than my vertical grammar, which is concerned specifically with grammatical relationships between two or more elements in different parallel poetic lines. Verticality is, on the other hand, a quite natural term for a compound sentence (CS) or a complex sentence (XC) whose clauses are divided into two poetic lines by scansion. The term is suited not only for the relationship between two or more parallel lines but also for the strophic constructions.

4.1. Vertical Grammar in Bicolons

The vertical grammatical relation between two parallel lines can easily be seen in a bicolon in which the two lines constitute a simple sentence (SS). One example, besides Ps 18:41, Hab 3:16a, and Mic 7:3b, is Ps 2:6, which shows rhyme as an instance of phonetic parallelism:

    a   b   c
waʾănî nāsaktî malkî
ʿal-ṣiyôn har-qodšî
    d   D′

I have installed my king
on Zion, my holy mountain.

While some may not consider these two lines parallel, I regard them as constituting a parallelism with a rhyme *malkî // qodšî* (-*î //* - *î*), that is, a phonetic parallelism, noting the alliteration of /i:/ as well as the assonance of /ʿal/ – /har/.[1] Here the first line (SVO) holds a vertical grammatical relationship with the second line (PP).

Such vertical grammatical relationships are also recognizable in other bicolons. Consider, for instance, Hab 2:1b, which has a structure a↓–x // x′–b↑, with a VG relationship a–b:

   a↓   x
   lirʾôt mah-yədabber-bî
   ûmâ ʾāšîb ʿal-tôkaḥtî
   x′   b↑

This text has been analyzed as a–b // b′–c′ and translated:

to see what he will say to me
and what I will answer concerning my complaint. (ESV)

In other words, c′ ("concerning my complaint") is usually thought to modify only the preceding verb "answer" *horizontally*. However, more recent translations emend *ʾāšîb* to *yāšîb* "he will answer" (so NRSV, REB),[2] apparently because they think it strange that the prophet would respond to his own complaint.

However, I analyze this bicolon as a↓–x // y–b↑, in which a and b hold a vertical grammatical relationship:

to see (a) what he will say to me (x)
and what I shall respond (y) concerning my complaint (b).

The phrases "what he will say to me" (x) and "what I shall respond" (rather than "answer") (y) constitute two sides of a dialogue, hence a merismus.[3]

---

1. For similar examples of a phonetic parallelism, see Song 5:1, 2, etc., on pp. 41–42, above.

2. Also BHS apparatus, following the Syriac. See also J. J. M. Roberts, *Nahum, Habakkuk, and Zephaniah*, OTL (Louisville: Westminster John Knox, 1991), 105. However, Robert D. Haak accepts *ʾāšîb*, translating "I will reply," though he adopts the translation "my prosecutor" for *tôkaḥtî*; see his *Habakkuk*, VTSup 44 (Leiden: Brill, 1992), 49.

3. For other examples, see Job 5:15 a↓–x // x′–b↑; SS, VG: a–b (V–O), Job 5:25 A–B (a–x) // B′ (x′–b); XS, VG: a–b (P–Adv), Job 6:9 a↓–x // b↑–x′.

4. Vertical Grammar in Parallelism

Let us consider also Hab 3:6a, which has the structure a↓-x // b↑-x′, with a VG relationship a–b:

a↓   x
ʿāmad waymōded ʾereṣ
rāʾâ wayyattēr gôyīm
b↑   x′

This text is usually analyzed as a–b–c // a′–b′–c′ and translated as follows:

> He stood, and shook the earth;
> he looked, and made the nations tremble. (NIV)

However, one could also say that verb "he stood" (a) is most closely related to the verb "he looked" (b) in the second line, while "he made the nations tremble" (x′) in the second line is a restatement of "he shook the earth" (x) in the first. Hence, the parallel structure is better taken as a–x // b–x′, a and b having a vertical grammatical relationship, and translated as follows:

> When he stood (a) [and] looked (b),
> he made the earth shake (x) and nations tremble (x′).

Vertical grammar also helps us to solve some long-standing *cruces* of exegesis, such as Hab 1:16:

ʿal-kēn yəzabbēaḥ ləḥermô
wîqaṭṭēr [piel] ləmikmartô

> Therefore he sacrifices to his net
> and burns incense[4] to his dragnet. (NIV)

> Therefore he sacrifices to his net
> and makes offerings[5] to his seine. (NRSV)

---

4. Also 2 Kgs 12:3; 14:4; 15:4, 35; 16:4; Isa 65:3; Hos 11:2; 2 Chr 28:4; see Roberts, *Nahum, Habakkuk, and Zephaniah*, 100.

5. NRSV translates the verb as "to offer incense" in Isa 65:3 and Hos 11:2 ("they kept sacrificing to the Baals, and offering incense to idols").

> Offering sacrifices to their nets
> and burning offerings[6] to their trawls. (REB)

These translations seem to reflect an analysis of the parallelism as a – b // a' – b'. The issue here is whether the text refers to two different actions or one set of sequential actions. If we take the verbal form, *piel* of *qṭr*, as implying burning incense, we might admit the former possibility. However, it now seems likely that the *hiphil* form rather than the *piel* was used to describe the burning of incense,[7] so the second possibility is the better solution. Since we should probably take these two lines (also in Hos 11:2) as expressing one thought, following the principle of "one thought through two lines," I propose that we take the two verbs as expressing two actions (as in 1 Kgs 22:44; 2 Kgs 12:3; 14:4; 15:4, 35; 16:4; 2 Chr 28:4) of a sacrificial rite: "to offer a sacrifice" (a) and "to have it go up in smoke"[8] (b). The parallelism could be analyzed as a↓-x // b↑-x', rather than a–b // a'–b':

> Therefore he offers a sacrifice to his net
> and lets it go up in smoke to his dragnet.

The parallelism as a whole can be paraphrased as, "Therefore he offers a sacrifice and burns it to his net/dragnet."

Another example is offered by Ps 24:6, a simple sentence with the structure a↓-x // x'-b↑ and a VG relationship a–b (cstr chain):

>   a↓   x
> *zeh dôr dōrəšāw*
> *məbaqšê pāneykā yaʿăqōb*
>   X'   b↑

Literally this is:

> Such is the generation (a) those who seek him (x)
> those who seek your face (X') Jacob (b)

---

6. REB translates the verb as "to burn incense" in Isa 65:3.
7. Diana Vikander Edelman, "The Meaning of *qiṭṭēr*," *VT* 35 (1985): 400.
8. According to Edelman ("The Meaning of *qiṭṭēr*," 395), the verb refers to "the act of burning the *'iššîm* portions of a sacrifice."; Haak (*Habakkuk*, 49; cf. *HALOT*, 1094–95) simply translates: "he sacrifices to his net and burns to his seine."

4. Vertical Grammar in Parallelism

I would translate it

> Such is the generation (a) of Jacob (b),
> those who seek him (x), that is, who seek your face (x').

I treated this text in "A Literary Insertion (AXB pattern) in Biblical Hebrew," a paper presented at the 1981 World Congress of Jewish Studies in Jerusalem.[9] At that time I was considering the literary phenomena of breakup and insertion. Here I would like to discuss this text as an example of vertical grammar.

In this long-standing *crux interpretatum*, the construct chain *dôr yaʿăqōb* "the generation of Jacob"[10] (ab) is broken up by the insertion of the parallel phrases *dōrəšāw* "those who seek him" and *məbaqšê pāneykā* "those who seek your face" (x // x').

Thus it is an example of an AXB pattern where "the generation (A) of Jacob (B)" is split by the insertion of X, the parallel phrases x // x'. This may also be analyzed as an example of vertical grammar, a↓-x // x' -b↑—

> *zeh dôr* (a) *dōrəšāw* (x)
> *məbaqšê pāneykā* (x') *yaʿăqōb* (b)

—in which a (*dôr*) and b (*yaʿăqōb*) have a vertical dependency, that is, are parts of the complement, a construct chain, ("the generation of Jacob") preceded by the subject *zeh* ("this"), while x' (*məbaqšê pāneykā*) is simply a rephrasing of x (*dōrəšāw*) in the parallelism. This is a chiasmus of the more often attested pattern a–x // b–x' noted above.

The next example, Hab 3:13b, has never been explained satisfactorily, so scholars typically ended up emending the text in order to come up with a reasonable meaning. However, I believe that vertical grammar can provide the clue to understanding the Hebrew text as it is. The structure of Hab 3:13b is a↓-x // y-b↑, with a VG relationship a–b, x–y:

---

9. Tsumura, "Literary Insertion (AXB Pattern) in Biblical Hebrew," 471–72.
10. For similar examples, see *dôr ṣaddîq* "the generation of the righteous" (Ps 14:5), *dôr ʾăbôtāyw* "the generation of his fathers" (49:20), *dôr yəšārîm* "the generation of the upright" (112:2); also Ugaritic *dr. il* (*KTU* 1.15.iii.19) "the generation of El."

       a↓   x
māḥaṣtā rōʾš mibbêt rāšāʿ
ʿārôt yəsôd ʿad-ṣawwāʾr
       y   b↑

Literally, this is:

> You crushed the head of the house of the wicked,
> laying bare the foundation to the neck.

It has been translated variously.

> You crushed the head of the house of the wicked,
>   laying him bare from thigh to neck. (ESV)

> You crushed the leader of the land of wickedness,
>   you stripped him from head to foot. (NIV)

> You will smash the roof of the villain's house,
> Raze it from foundation to top. (JPS)

All these translations take the text as a bicolon in which each line has a horizontal grammar: for example, in the first line taking *mibbêt rāšāʿ* as modifying the preceding term *rōʾš* ("head," "leader," or "roof"), and in the second line taking the phrase *ʿad-ṣawwāʾr* (lit. "to the neck") as modifying the preceding term *yəsôd* "foundation." However, since the terms "head" and "neck" are in the same semantic field, as are "house" and "foundation," it seems that the lines are parallel. However, since in Hebrew neither line makes sense by itself without emendation, one might suspect that those terms are related vertically to each other. In the light of the verticality of Hebrew poetry, I suggest that the bicolon has a structure of a↓-x↓ // y↑-b↑, in which a is vertically related to b and x is vertically related to y. With this understanding, the text would be translated as a–b // x–y:

> You crushed the head (a) to the neck (b),
> from the house of the wicked (x) laying the foundation bare (y).

With x+y, God is depicted as totally destroying the enemy's palace, even "laying the foundation bare." With a+b, God is depicted as a victorious warrior who crushes the enemy's head with a mace and then cuts off the head, making the corpse "up to the neck," as is often depicted in Assyrian battle reliefs. In the light of x+y, it may in particular be describing the destruction of the statue of the enemy king (or god) by making it headless in its house, as was often practiced in a conquered city.

The following examples can be explained along similar lines. For example, Isa 64:10b is a simple sentence with the structure x–a↓–y // x'–b↑, in which x // x' and the VG relationship is ab (cstr chain).

   x   a↓   y
ṣiyôn midbār hāyātâ
yərûšālaim šəmāmâ
   x'   b↑

Zion has become a wilderness,
Jerusalem a desolation. (ESV)

The issue in translating this parallelism is whether it should be taken as a compound sentence or a simple sentence. In the former, the translation would be:

Zion has become a wilderness;
Jerusalem [has become] a desolation.

Here "Zion" and "Jerusalem" are coreferential, and the parallelism seems synonymous. Hence, the meaning of this bicolon should be taken something like, "Zion Jerusalem has become a wilderness and a desolation." However, since the term *midbār* for "wilderness" (m.) and the term *šəmāmāh* for "desolation" (f.) often form a construct chain *midbār šəmāmāh* "a desolate wilderness" (lit. "a wilderness of desolation"; Jer 12:10, Joel 2:3, 3:19 [MT 4:19]), it is reasonable to take these two terms as holding a vertical grammatical relationship. If this is the case, the bicolon constitutes a simple sentence with the following meaning:

Zion Jerusalem has become a wilderness of desolation.

A final example is provided by Ps 2:4, a compound sentence with the structure X–a↓ // x'–a'–b↑, in which X // x' and a // a' (hendiadys), with a VG relationship ab.

    X   a↓
  yôšēb baššāmayim yiśḥāq
  'ădōnāy yil'ag-lāmô
  x' a' b↑

He who sits in the heavens laughs;
the Lord scoffs at them.

Here a compound sentence is made up of two poetic lines. However, the two verbs "to laugh" and "to scoff" should not be treated separately. They are a verbal hendiadys distributed vertically in two different lines. Consequently, they mean "to laugh and scoff" and take "them" (*lāmô*) as their object. Therefore, it is misleading to translate the first clause as an autonomous poetic line: "He who sits in the heavens laughs." The meaning of this bicolon should be: "He who sits in the heavens, that is, the Lord, laughs and scoffs at them."

4.2. Vertical Grammar in Tricolons

Just as there is verticality in bicolons, we can also see verticality in tricolons. For example, Ps 19:14 is a simple sentence with the structure A↓–x // X'–b↑ // C↑ and a VG relation a–b:

 yihyû lərāṣôn 'imrê-pî
   A↓   x
 wəhegyôn libbî ləpāneykā
   X'   b↑
 YHWH ṣûrî wəgō'ălî
    C↑

May the words of my mouth (x) and the meditation of my heart (X') be acceptable (A) in your sight (b),
O LORD, my rock and my redeemer (C).

The two subjects, "the words of my mouth" (x) and "the meditation of my heart" (X'), are in the first two lines and constitute a merismus. These two noun phrases, being an enjambment,[11] *as a whole* serve as the subject of

---

11. For this phenomenon, see chapter 5.

the verbal phrase "May they be acceptable" (A: *yihyû lərāṣôn*) in the first line. The prepositional phrase "before you" (b: *ləpāneykā*) in the second line is vertically dependent on the verbal phrase in the first line. Moreover, the vocatives *YHWH ṣûrî wəgōʾălî* in the third line are certainly related vertically to the pronominal suffix ("your") in the second line. Thus the grammatical features of verticality are recognizable in the poetic parallelism of this simple sentence. Note the phonetic parallelism with the assonances of *-î // -î // -î -î, -ôn // -ôn* in the three lines.

Another example is provided by Ps 18:11 [12], a simple sentence with the structure a–b–x // C–x' // B'–B" and the VG relation a–b–c.[12]

yāšet ḥōšek sitrô
   a   b   x
səbîbôtāyw sukkātô
     C   x'
ḥeškat-mayim ʿābê šəḥāqîm
    B'   B"

He made darkness his covering,
around him his canopy,
darkness of waters, thick clouds of the skies.

This verse differs structurally from its parallel 2 Sam 22:12; the latter is a bicolon, while the former is a tricolon.

Ps 18:11
He made (a) darkness (b) his covering (x),
around him (c) his canopy (x'),
the darkness of waters (B'), thick clouds of the skies (B").

2 Sam 22:12
And he made (a) darkness (b) around him (c) *his* canopies (x),
the sieve of waters (B'), thick clouds of the skies (B").

The phrase "thick clouds of the skies" (*ʿābê šəḥāqîm*; also Ps 18:11) in 2 Sam 22:12 has been taken as a gloss,[13] but the structures of two parallel

---

12. See above, p. 17.
13. E.g., P. Kyle McCarter Jr., *II Samuel: A New Translation with Introduction, Notes, and Commentary*, AB 9 (Garden City, NY: Doubleday, 1984), 457.

passages support that it existed in the original. A comparison of the first line of 2 Sam 22:12 and the first two lines of Ps 18:11 suggests that the colon (or line) is expanded into a bicolon, with the addition of the parallel term "his covering." Here the grammatical relation between "he made darkness" and "around him" is *horizontal* in 2 Sam 22:12, while in Ps 18:11 it is *vertical* with the structure a–b–x // C–x', in which a–b–c constitutes a vertical grammar of SVOX.[14]

Let us look also at Ps 2:2, a compound sentence with a coreferential subject, the structure a↓–x // x'–a' // B↑, and a VG relation of a–B (V–PP).

yityaṣṣəbû malkê-'ereṣ
   a↓   x
wərôzənîm nôsədû-yāḥad
   x'   a'
ʿ*al-YHWH wəʿal-məšîḥô*
       B↑

The kings of the earth set themselves,
and the rulers take counsel together,
against the Lord and against his Anointed, saying.... (ESV)

All modern versions translate the preposition ʿ*al* as "against" in both places in the third line and take the preposition as modifying vertically the directly preceding verbal phrase "take counsel together" (*nôsədû-yāḥad*) in the second line.

However, in view of the verbal phrase "to stand before/by the presence of/beside" (*yṣb*, hitpael + ʿ*al*) found in passages such as Num 23:3, 15; Zech 6:5; Job 1:6; 2:1; and 2 Chr 11:13, it is better to take the two prepositional phrases ʿ*al-YHWH wəʿal-məšîḥô* as modifying the verb *yityaṣṣəbû* in the first line. In other words, in this tricolon the third line has a *vertical* grammatical relation with the first line. Hence, I suggest the following translation, though the English word order has to be changed:

[Why do][15] the kings of the earth (x), namely, the rulers (x'), stand (a)

---

14. A (he made darkness) and B (around him) have a vertical grammatical relationship, while on the other hand X' (his canopy) is simply a restatement of X (his covering). See Tsumura, "Vertical Grammar of Parallelism in Hebrew Poetry," 167–81.

15. "Why" (*lāmmâ*) in v. 1 functions double-duty.

before the Lord and before his anointed (B)
and yet take counsel together (a').

Another tricolon that also constitutes a simple sentence is Hab 3:8a. It has the structure x–a–b // x'–c // x"–c and a VG relationship a–b–c.

hăbinhārîm ḥārāh YHWH
    x   a↓   b
'im bannəhārîm 'appekā
    x'   c↑
'im-bayyām 'ebrātekā
    x"   c'↑

Against the rivers (x) does burn (a), O Lord (b),
against the rivers (x') your anger (c),
or against the sea (x") your rage (c')?

This tricolon can be reduced to a simple prose sentence:

Against the rivers (x = x') or against the sea (x") does your anger (c), namely, your rage (c'), burn (a), O Lord (b)?

The first two lines (3:8a) constitute a bicolon, and the third line is simply a restatement of the second. The verb *ḥārāh* (a: "it burns": *qal* pf 3ms) in the first line and its subject *'appekā* (c: "your anger": m.) in the second have a vertical grammatical relationship, thus "your anger burns" (a–c). On the other hand, *'im bannəhārîm* (x') in the second line is simply a restatement of *hăbinhārîm* (x) in the first line.

Another example is Hab 1:7b, a simple sentence with the structure a↓–x // x'–b↑ and the VG relation a–b.

'āyōm wənôrā' hû'
    a↓   x
mimmennû mišpāṭô
ûś'ētô yēṣē'
  x' b↑

Some translate this verse as a bicolon:

> They are dreaded and fearsome;
> their justice and dignity go forth from themselves (ESV; also NRSV)

Others, however, translate it as a tricolon:

> They are a feared and dreaded people;
> they are a law to themselves
> and promote their own honor. (NIV11)

Formally, this verse is better analyzed as a tricolon with 3:2:2 [6:6:6], as in the NIV11, rather than as the very unbalanced bicolon with 3:4 [6:12]. However, while NIV11 takes the last two lines as a compound sentence, I take them as constituting a simple sentence, the prepositional phrase *mimmennû* (a) modifying the verb *yēṣēʾ* (b) vertically. The subject (x) in the second line is replaced by another subject (x′) in the third line, hence the pattern a↓–x // x′–b↑, with a vertical grammar relationship between a and b and with x′ a restatement of x:

> Out of themselves [lit. him] (a) their judgment (x),
> *namely*, their decree (x′), goes forth (b).

ESV and NRSV seem to take *mimmennû mišpāṭô ûśʾētô yēṣēʾ* as a single line, translating "their *justice and dignity* go forth from themselves" (emphasis added). The verticality in the last two lines rather suggests the meaning, "their judgment, namely, their decree, goes [sg.] forth out of themselves." This view is supported also by the collocation of the term *mišpāṭ* with the verb *yṣʾ* "to go out"; see, for example, Hab 1:4: "justice does not go forth"; Ps 17:2: "may my vindication come from you."[16]

4.3. Vertical Grammar in AXX′B Tetracolons[17]

There are also some examples of vertical grammar in four-line parallelisms. Previously I noted such examples as inserted bicolon (e.g., Ps 9:6; Amos 1:5), focusing on the inserted elements, the middle two lines of a

---

16. For further examples, see §4.3, below.
17. Tsumura, "Vertical Grammar of Biblical Hebrew Parallelism," 447–59.

four-line parallelism. My focus here is on the grammatical relationship between the first line (A) and the fourth line (B) of an AXX'B tetracolon. The outer lines (i.e., A // B) depend each other vertically and could be considered as a kind of an enjambment, a "distant enjambment." However, the term *enjambment* suggests scansion, not a grammatical aspect. We are concerned with the vertical grammatical dependency between A and B.[18]

We begin with Ps 9:6 (MT 9:7):

A↓   hāʾôyēb tammû
X   ḥŏrābôt lāneṣaḥ
X'   wəʿārîm nātaštā
B↑   ʾābad zikrām hēmmāh

The enemy are destroyed,
  —as ruins forever,
    cities you have uprooted—
even the memory of them has perished.[19]

One might note that this pattern AXX'B is different from the patterns AXX'A' (envelope type), ABB'A' (mirror image), and AXYA', which are basically variations on the ABA pattern. While in all of these the first and last lines are a parallel bicolon in Ps 9:6, as in Amos 1:5 (below), the first and last lines depend each other grammatically but are not parallel.

The pattern AXX'B does exist in the following examples, in which two sets of bicolons seemingly constitute a tetracolon.

4.3.1. Amos 1:5

A↓   wəšābartî bərîaḥ dammeśeq
X   wəhikrattî yôšēb mibbiqʿat-ʾāwen
X'   wətômēk šēbeṭ mibbêt ʿeden
B↑   wəgālû ʿam-ʾărām qîrāh

---

18. See Watson, *Classical Hebrew Poetry*, 332–35. See also F. W. Dobbs-Allsopp, *On Biblical Poetry* (Oxford: Oxford University Press, 2015), 45–46, 148, etc.; for segmentation with reference to line, see 90–94.

19. Tsumura, "'Inserted Bicolon,' the AXYB Pattern," 235–36.

And I will shatter the bar of Damascus,
    and I will cut off the enthroned one from the Valley of Aven,
    and him who holds the scepter from Beth-eden,
and the people of Aram shall go into exile to Kir.

Here the lines X and X' constitute a typical synonymous bicolon with a ballast variant in X'. However, the first line (A) and the last line (B) have a vertical grammatical relation; that is, the last line (B) is grammatically dependent on the first (A) and logically the result of it, hence the complex sentence:

Since I will shatter the bar of Damascus,
the people of Aram shall go into exile to Kir.

Therefore, this is an AXX'B pattern in which the first and last lines, A and B, are dependent on each other vertically.[20]

4.3.2. Job 12:24–25

    A↓   *mēsîr lēb rāʾšê ʿam-hāʾāreṣ*
    X   *wayyatʿēm bətōhû lōʾ-dārek*
    X'   *yəmašəšû-ḥōšek wəlōʾ-ʾôr*
    B↑   *wayyatʿēm kaššikkôr*

Taking away understanding from the chiefs of the people of the earth,
    and he makes them wander in a trackless waste;
        they grope in the dark without light.
He makes them stagger like a drunken man.

Here the middle two lines constitute a good two-line parallelism with the word pair "waste" (*tōhû*) and "the dark" (*ḥōšek*), a pair we find in Gen 1:2 and Jer 4:23.[21] On the other hand, the first and last lines have a grammatical relation: the first line (A) is a participle phrase that modifies the main

---

    20. This is different from the envelope pattern AXX'A' and the mirror pattern ABB'A'. In these patterns, the first and last lines are a parallel bicolon. However, in the above case the first and last lines are related grammatically but are not parallel.
    21. Tsumura, *Creation and Destruction*, 27 n. 98, 29.

clause (B) vertically. So this is also a case of an inserted bicolon AXX'B rather than a mirror image ABB'A'.

4.3.3. 2 Sam 3:33b–34c

> *hakkəmôt nābāl yāmût ʾAbnēr*
> *yādekā lōʾ-ʾăsūrôt wəragleykā*
> *lōʾ-linḥuštayim huggāšû*
> *kinpôl lipnê bənê-ʿawlāh nāpāltā*

> Like a fool dies should Abner die?
> Neither your hands nor your feet were bound;
> they were not put in fetters.
> Like a falling before sons of injustice have you fallen?

According to the MT scansion, the second and third lines of this tetracolon elegy (3:334a–b) are divided as follows:

yādekā lōʾ-ʾăsūrôt	2 (7)
wəragleykā lōʾ-linḥuštayim huggāšû	3 (12)

> Your hands were not bound;
> your feet were not fettered.

However, this scansion is metrically unbalanced. Thus P. Kyle McCarter, David Noel Freedman, A. A. Anderson, and Elishaʿ Qimron all add "by manacles" (*bzqym*) or "in chains" after the first clause, based on 4QSam[a], *bzqym*, to improve the balance within the parallelism.[22] However, one can scan the lines like BHS as follows:

---

22. McCarter, *II Samuel*, 111; David Noel Freedman, "On the Death of Abner," in *Love and Death in the Ancient Near East: Essays in Honor of Marvin H. Pope*, ed. John H. Marks and Robert M. Good (Guilford, CT: Four Quarters, 1987), 125–27; A. A. Anderson, *2 Samuel*, WBC 11 (Dallas: Word, 1989), 52, 54; Elishaʿ Qimron, "The Lament of David over Abner," in *Birkat Shalom: Studies in the Bible, Ancient Near Eastern Literature, and Postbiblical Judaism Presented to Shalom M. Paul on the Occasion of His Seventieth Birthday*, ed. Chaim Cohen et al. (Winona Lake, IN: Eisenbrauns, 2008), 1:143–47.

yādekā lō'-'ăsūrôt wəragleykā	3 (11)
lō'-linḥuštayim huggāšû[23]	2 (8)

Your hands were not bound and your feet;
they were not put in fetters.

The line *yādekā lō'-'ăsūrôt wəragleykā* is an example of interrupted coordination, the AX and B pattern in which A and B "your hands and your feet" (*yādekā wəragleykā*) is interrupted by the insertion of X "were not bound" (*lō'-'ăsūrôt*) to mean, "Neither your hands nor your feet were bound," similar to Ps 11:5a ("The LORD tests the righteous and the wicked"; so NRSV, NASB).[24] In this understanding, the "and" of "and your feet" (so MT, 4QSam^a) is necessary rather than being an additional conjunction (cf. "your feet" in McCarter).

One might take the interrogative *h-* in the first line (3:33b) as modifying the fourth line (3:34c) as well: "…have you fallen?" // "…should Abner die?" Thus this four-line parallelism constitutes an AXYB pattern in which the middle two lines are an inserted bicolon, as in Ps 17:1 and Job 12:24–25.[25] Note that the inserted bicolon here has the *qinah* pattern, which is the most suitable with the 3:2 scansion for a lament (see 2 Sam 18:33).

A↓	Like a fool dies should Abner die?	4
X	Neither your hands nor your feet were bound;	3
X'	they were not put in fetters.	2
B↑	Like a falling before sons of injustice have you fallen?	4

4.3.4. Ps 89:36–37 (MT 37–38)

A↓	*zar'ô lə'ôlām yihyeh*	3
X	*wəkis'ô kaššemeš negdî*	3
X'	*kəyārēaḥ yikkôn 'ôlām*	3
B↑	*wə'ēd baššaḥaq ne'ĕmān*	3

---

23. Pual "were brought near" (lit.). 4QSam^a has *hg* [*y*]*š* (see Edward D. Herbert, *Reconstructing Biblical Dead Sea Scrolls: A New Method Applied to the Reconstruction of 4QSam^a* [Leiden: Brill, 1997], 113), not *hgš* (McCarter, *II Samuel*, 111).
24. See Tsumura, "Coordination Interrupted," 117–32.
25. See David Toshio Tsumura, *The First Book of Samuel*, NICOT (Grand Rapids: Eerdmans, 2007), 61–63.

His offspring shall be forever;
   his throne is like the sun before me;
   like the moon it shall be established forever,
as a faithful witness in the clouds.

This tetracolon is often interpreted as consisting of two bicolons and translated as two sentences. The NIV even has the fourth line appositive to "moon" in the third line, which is impossible.

Here again it is better to take the middle two lines as constituting a typical synonymous parallelism with the word pair "the sun" and "the moon." Two outside lines constitute a vertical parallelism, in which the last line is grammatically dependent on the first line. Thus:

His offspring shall be forever,
as a faithful witness in the clouds.[26]

So this is the case of one bicolon inserted in another, AXX′B, not a bicolon followed by its mirror image, ABB′A′.

Note that the fourth line constitutes an AXB pattern[27] in which the phrase "in the skies" interrupts the composite unit "a faithful witness," a phrase found in Jer 42:5 ("a true and faithful witness") and Rev 3:14 ("the faithful and true witness") and 19:11 ("Faithful and True"; cf. Isa 8:2: "reliable witnesses").[28]

4.3.5. Song 5:5

Let us look at Song 5:5, which has a slightly different structure.

   A↓   *qamtî ʾănî liptōaḥ lədôdî*
   X   *wəyāday nāṭəpû-môr*
   X′   *wəʾeṣbəʿōtay môr ʿōbēr*
   B↑   *ʿal kappôt hammanʿûl*

I arose to open to my beloved,
and my hands dripped with myrrh,

---

26. Rev. 1:7: "he is coming in the clouds."
27. Tsumura, "Literary Insertion (AXB Pattern) in Biblical Hebrew," 468–82.
28. See also Ps 17:1, Isa 35:4, Hos 11:10, Mic 2:4, and Hab 3:13b.

my fingers with liquid myrrh,
upon the handles of the bolt. (NRSV)

Some scholars interpret this text as having a sexual symbolism, assuming that the word "hands" refers to the "male member," despite the fact that "hands" is plural and the hands and fingers are those of the woman.[29] One should certainly grasp the literal meaning of the text grammatically before interpreting metaphorically or assuming poetic exaggeration (hyperbole) or the like.

It is clear that the second and the third lines are a perfect parallel in which "hands" and "fingers" correspond to each other[30] and "myrrh" in the second line is further specified by "liquid myrrh" in the third. On the other hand, the fourth line has given rise to many different interpretations.

Usually it is held that the preposition ʿal of the fourth line modifies the immediately preceding verbal form ʿōbēr of the third line. Hess, for example, thinks that the myrrh "flows off her body onto the bolt and its guides, which she touches."[31] Keel similarly explains that "the myrrh is on the handles of the bolt used to lock the door." However, since he holds that the text has no parallel to the phrase "upon the handles of the bolt," the fourth line is a gloss.[32] Pope, on the other hand, explains this liquid myrrh on the door bolt as "tokens left by disappointed lovers," such as flowers, wine, verses, or perfume.[33]

However, the fourth line (b) seems rather to depend vertical-grammatically on the first line (a). In other words, the preposition ʿal modifies the verbal form liptōaḥ "to open" in the first line, thus "to open by (or at) the handles[34] of the bolt." The entire tetracolon constitutes an AXX'B pat-

---

29. Duane A. Garrett, *Proverbs, Ecclesiastes, Song of Songs*, NAC (Nashville: Broadman, 1993). However, in West Semitic languages, *yad* is singular when it is used euphemistically for the male member; see, for example, the Ugaritic text *KTU* 1.23:33–35. Michael V. Fox (*The Song of Songs and the Ancient Egyptian Love Songs* [Madison: University of Wisconsin Press, 1985], 144–45) rejects the idea that it is a sexual metaphor in this text.

30. "Hands" and "fingers" are a word pair common to Ugaritic and Hebrew; see Pope, *Song of Songs*, 521.

31. Hess, *Song of Songs*, 173.

32. Keel, *The Song of Songs*, 193. The Vulgate ends the sentence with the second *môr* and and begins a new sentence, "I opened the bolt...." See Pope, *Song of Songs*, 521.

33. Pope, *Song of Songs*, 523.

34. For a similar phrase, note "at the soles of your feet" (ʿal-kappôt raglayik) in Isa 60:14. Cf. *kappôt yād* "in the hollow of the hand" (1 Sam 5:4; 2 Kgs 9:35; Dan 10:10).

tern in which a bicolon, X//X', is inserted between another bicolon, A//B. The meaning of the four-line parallelism is as follows:

> I arose to open for my beloved by (or at) the handles of the bolt; (A//B)
> my hands, even my fingers, dripped with myrrh, with liquid myrrh. (X//X')

However, when she opened the door she found that he had already gone away (5:6)![35]

This phenomenon of the AXX'B pattern can be recognized also in the final verse in the Song, 8:14:

> A↓ bərah dôdî
> X   ûdmēh-ləkā lişbî
> X' 'ô ləʿōper hāʾayyālîm
> B↑ ʿal hārê bəśāmîm

> Escape, my beloved!
>   And be like a gazelle
>   or a young stag
> toward[36] the mountains of spice!

Almost all English translations take the first term to mean a quick movement, as reflected in translations such as "to make haste" (KJV, RSV, NRSV, ESV), "to hurry" (NASB, JPS), and "to haste away" (NJB). However, the verb means "to run away, flee, escape" and refers literally to a physical movement from a location A to a location B in this context, rather than to do some action quickly, as in the case of *mhr* (*piel*).

As in the previous example, the prepositional phrase (ʿ*al hārê bəśāmîm*) of the fourth line (B) depends vertically on the verb *bərah* in the first line (A) rather than modifying the immediately preceding noun

---

35. Lawrence E. Stager claims that a fist-sized keyhole in the door is alluded to here; see "Key Passages," *Eretz-Israel* 27 (2003): 241*. One should note, however, that the hand in the figure he includes is that of a person outside. In this poem the woman opened the door *by the handle(s)* from the inside.

36. A classical example of the preposition ʿ*al* "toward" or "to" rather than "on" or "against" is 2 Kgs 23:29; for other examples, see *HALOT*, s.v.

"a young stag" (*ʿōper hāʾayyālîm*). The third line (X′) with a ballast variant *ʿōper hāʾayyālîm* for *ṣbî* of the second is certainly a restatement of the second line (X). The meaning of the entire parallelism is as follows:

> Escape, my beloved, toward the mountains of spice   (A//B)
> and be like a gazelle or a young stag!   (X//X′)

Thus the passage constitutes an AXX′B pattern, just like 5:5. Such a pattern, which includes the phenomenon of "inserted bicolon," is also attested in Amos 1:5, Ps 9:6, Hab 3:13b, Hos 11: 10, Isa 35:4, Ps 17: 1, Mic 2:4, and Job 12:24–25.[37]

With this understanding of the grammar and parallelism, one can proceed to a better grasp of the metaphor in this passage. The female lover here urges her beloved to go away toward the mountains of spice, presumably the place where she is, so that he may act there like a young stag. While a formal analysis in terms of grammar and parallelism may not provide a clear-cut explanation of a highly elevated metaphor, it still directs the readers to the simple fact that the emphasis is on the location, "the mountain of spice," and on how he would act there with his lover.

4.4. Vertical Grammar in ABXB′ Tetracolons[38]

Among the Chinese literary techniques taken into Japanese is the well-known *ki-shô-ten-ketsu* (起承転結), which one can translate as "statement–development–twist–denouement" (or "introduction, development, turn, and conclusion"). The famous historian and poet Rai Sanyô 頼山陽 (1780–1832) used the following example to illustrate this technique.

起　「京の三条」糸屋の娘
承　姉は十六妹十四

---

37. For other examples of the inserted bicolon in Hebrew poetry, see Tsumura, "'Inserted Bicolon,' the AXYB Pattern," 234–36; Tsumura, "Coordination Interrupted," 117–32, esp. 130.

38. David Toshio Tsumura, "Statement–Development–Twist–Denouement: The AA′XB Pattern in Biblical Hebrew Poetry," in *Prince of the Orient: A Memorial Volume for H. I. H. Prince Takahito Mikasa*, ed. Ichiro Nakata et al. Orient Supplement 1 (Tokyo: Near Eastern Studies in Japan, 2019), 269–72.

転　諸国諸大名は弓矢で殺す
結　娘二人は目で殺す

The daughters of a thread merchant of Sanjo in Kyoto;
the elder was sixteen, the younger fourteen.
The lords of the provinces kill by bow and arrow;
these daughters kill by their eyes.

The first line is an introduction of the theme ("the daughters of a thread merchant of Sanjo in Kyoto"); the second line is a development of the first, stating how old these girls were. At the third line, though, we find a sudden twist or turn of subject from "daughters" to "lords," creating tension. The fourth line, the denouement, concludes the poem, bringing back "the daughters" and connecting them with the "lords" of the third line.

A similar poetic technique is also found in Biblical Hebrew. Consider, for example, Ps 34:9–10 (MT 34:10–11).

A↓　yər(ʾ)û ʾet-YHWH qədōšāyw
B↑　kî-ʾên maḥsôr lîrēʾāyw
X 　kəpîrîm rāšû wərāʿēbû
B'　wədōrəšê YHWH lōʾ-yaḥsərû kol-ṭôb

O, fear the Lord, you his saints,
for those who fear him have no lack!
The young lions suffer want and hunger,
but those who seek the Lord lack no good thing.

These verses seem to constitute a tetracolon with the following structure:

Statement: Summons to fear the Lord
Development: for (= the reason I say this is that)[39] those who fear him have no lack.

---

39. Here the particle "for" (*kî*) does not express a direct cause-and-result relationship between two clauses. It functions rather as a speaker-oriented particle that explains the reason why the speaker stated the previous summons. See Walter T. Claasen, "Speaker-Oriented Functions of *ki* in Biblical Hebrew," *JNSL* 11 (1983): 29–46; David Toshio Tsumura, "The Speaker-Oriented Connective Particle ʿAl-Kēn in 2 Sam. 7:22," *JSS* 65 (2020): 85–91.

Twist: The young lions suffer want and hunger
Denouement: but those who seek the Lord lack no good thing.

The first two lines (a complex sentence), which depend on each other vertically, talk about fearing the Lord. Suddenly, however, a completely different topic (twist) appears, that of young lions. However, the fourth line resumes the initial theme: fear and seek the Lord.

The rhetorical pattern of these four lines can be analyzed as an ABXB' pattern, where a sudden twist or turn (X) is inserted within a tricolon ABB', interrupting the flow of the parallelism. Here this element X is clearly a sudden twist from people to lions and creates tension, as the line of thought is not clear. Of course, the audience knows that a young lion is dangerous and powerful. But in the last line the connection with the first part is shown by expressing the contrast between a powerful but hungry lion and one who fears the Lord and lacks no good thing.

Amos 3:7–8 is another example that involves a lion in the twist.

⁷ kî lōʾ yaʿăśeh ʾădōnāy YHWH dābār
kî ʾim-gālāh sôdô ʾel-ʿăbādāyw hannəbîʾîm
⁸ ʾaryēh šāʾāg mî lōʾ yîrāʾ
ʾădōnāy YHWH dibber mî lōʾ yinnābēʾ

⁷ For the Lord God does not do anything
without revealing his secret to his servants, the prophets.
⁸ The lion has roared; who will not fear?
The Lord God has spoken; who can but prophesy?

A↓	Statement:	Introducing the theme: God does everything,
B↑	Development:	but first he reveals his secret to his prophets.
X	Twist:	If a lion roars, everybody fears;
B'	Denouement:	if God has spoken, every prophet must prophesy.

In this text there is a sudden *twist* in the flow of discourse from God and his prophets to a lion. A roaring lion naturally causes people to fear, so one must react to its roar. In the last line this roar is connected with the prophets by pointing out that the authoritative voice of the Lord means that no prophet can avoid prophesying. A lion as a metaphor for the authoritative voice of the Lord also occurs at the beginning of the book: "The Lord roars from Zion / and utters his voice from Jerusalem" (1:2).

The vertical structure of these four lines is again an ABXB' pattern in which the A line and the B line constitute vertical grammar and the X line, inserted between B and B', interrupts the flow of discourse and creates tension.

My third example, Hab 2:4–5a, has many exegetical problems. ESV even notes that the meaning of the Hebrew of 5a is uncertain. However, I believe that the problem can be solved if we recognize here the same tetracolon structure as above.

⁴ *hinnēh ʿuppəlâ lōʾ-yāšərâ napšô bô*
wəṣaddîq beʾĕmûnātô yiḥyeh
⁵ *wəʾap kî-hayyayin bôgēd*
geber yāhîr wəlōʾ yinweh

⁴ Behold, his soul is puffed up within him and not upright,
but the righteous shall live by his faith.
⁵ Moreover, wine is a traitor;
the man is arrogant and not at rest.

A basic question is whether verse 4 should be connected with the preceding verse ("wait for the vision") or with the following verse or should be treated independently. This is a hotly debated question. There is great variety among modern English translations in the range of the paragraph that includes verse 4: verses 1–5 (NRSV); 2–5 (NIV11); 4–5 (NASB, NIV, NEB); 4–8 (ASV); 3–5 (RSV); 4 (ESV, JB, NJB); 1–20 (JPS, REB).

Most translations, except for the last two groups, hold that verse 4 is connected with verse 5. Here I suggest, based on the parallel structure, that this is correct and that verses 4–5a should be taken as a four-line parallelism. When we take this as a unit, we can note the same structure of statement–development–twist–denouement as in the preceding two examples.

A↓ Statement: Introducing the theme: the wicked (man) is conceited.
B↑ Development: The righteous shall live by his trust on God.
X Twist: Wine is a traitor.
B' Denouement: The (wicked) man is arrogant.

From the context of Hab 1–2, it is reasonable to hold that the pronouns "his" and "him" refer to "the wicked" (*rāšāʿ*) of Hab 1:4 and 1:13. Hence, "the righteous" (*ṣaddîq*) in the second line is contrasted with "the wicked." But in the third line, the image of "wine" (*yyn*) suddenly appears, and this has been often taken as unsuitable to the context. The Habakkuk Dead Sea Scroll has "wealth" (*hwn*) instead of "wine," and some modern English translation adopt that word in this passage (NRSV, NJB).

However, the MT "wine," completely unexpected, twists the flow of discourse. The particle *wəʾap kî* ("moreover") appears in the beginning of verse 5: "Moreover, wine is a traitor." One may wonder why such a phrase would suddenly come here. However, in 1:13 "the wicked" are described as "traitors." So, although the third line begins with "Moreover wine...," the key word "traitor" reminds the audience/reader of "the wicked" whose soul is "not upright" of the first line. It should be noted that the term "traitors" is contrasted with "the upright" in Prov 12:3 and 12:6.

The final line concludes with a description of the restless and arrogant nature of the wicked man: *geber yāhîr wəlōʾ yinweh*. The image of "wine" would also lead the audience to recall the proverbial sayings:

lēṣ hayyayin hōmeh šēkār
wəkol-šōgeh bô lōʾ yeḥkām

Wine is a mocker, strong drink a brawler,
and whoever is led astray by it is not wise. (Prov 20:1 ESV)

zēd yāhîr lēṣ šəmô
ʿōśeh baʿebrat zādôn

"Scoffer" is the name of the arrogant, haughty man
who acts with arrogant pride. (Prov 21:24 ESV)

Thus the sudden appearance of the image of "wine" induces a tension that is resolved in the fourth line. Taking the MT text as it stands, one can appreciate the literary technique of the Hebrew prophets.

The rhetorical structure of these four lines is again an ABXB' pattern in which the A line and the B line constitute an antithetical parallelism and the X line, inserted between B and B', interrupts the flow of discourse and creates tension.

Thus the literary technique of statement–development–twist–denouement is an effective means of creating vividness and suspense in a poetic text that can be found in Biblical Hebrew as well as in Chinese and Japanese poetry. It has its origin in the universal principles of human languages and literary devices.

4.5. Verticality in Strophes

The verticality of grammar can be further recognized in strophes that consist of an accumulation of poetic lines, just as linearity of prose grammar in syntax can be seen in paragraphs, that is, in suprasentencial units of discourse. Consider, for example, Prov 3:5–10:

A↓   ⁵ *bəṭaḥ ʾel-YHWH bəkol-libbekā*
B↓   *wəʾel-bînātəkā ʾal-tiššāʿēn*
A'↓ ⁶ *bəkol-dərākeykā dāʿēhû*
C↑   *wəhûʾ yəyaššēr ʾōrəḥōteykā*

Trust in the LORD with all your heart,
and do not lean on your own understanding.
In all your ways acknowledge him,
and he will make straight your paths.

A↓   ⁷ *ʾal-təhî ḥākām bəʿêneykā*
B↓   *yərāʾ ʾet-YHWH wəsûr mērāʿ*
C↑   ⁸ *ripʾût təhî ləšārekā*
C' ↑ *wəšiqqûy ləʿaṣmôteykā*

Be not wise in your own eyes;
fear the LORD, and turn away from evil.
It will be healing to your flesh
and refreshment to your bones.

A ↓⁹ *kabbēd ʾet-YHWH mēhônekā*
A' ↓ *ûmērēʾšît kol-təbûʾāteykā*
B↑¹⁰ *wəyimmāləʾû ʾăsāmeykā śābāʿ*
B' ↑ *wətîrôš yəqābeykā yiprōṣû*

Honor the LORD with your wealth
and with the firstfruits of all your produce;
then your barns will be filled with plenty,
and your vats will be bursting with wine. (ESV)

In the above section, verse 6b (C↑) is subordinate[40] to the three imperative clauses in lines 5a-6a (A // B // A'). In verse 8 (C↑ // C'↑), the subject ("it") of the verb təhî is the set of commands in verse 7 "to be not wise" A↓ (v. 7a) as well as "to fear and turn" B↓ (v. 7b). In the third strophe, verse 10 (B↑ // B'↑) is the result clause for the main clause ("command") in verse 9 (A↓ // A'↓). One might even take the whole of verses 5–10 as one strophe, since similar commands such as "trust in the Lord," "fear the Lord," and "honor the Lord" are repeated in each of the four-line parallelisms: verses 5–6, 7–8, and 9–10.

---

40. See §1.3.2, above.

5
Syntax and Scansion in the Biblical Hebrew Poetry

The grammatical relationship within parallel structures is sometimes complicated, and in such cases scholars are often discouraged to detect the parallelisms. A poetic line with the prose particle *kî* is such a case. However, if one observes the *vertical* grammatical relationship between the two lines, such unusual cases may be explained as reasonable examples of Hebrew poetic parallelism.

5.1. Enjambment in Poetic Parallelism

The vertical grammar of parallelism appears to be related to the phenomenon of enjambment, where a single phrase is divided into two parts, one at the end of the first line and the other at the beginning of the second line. With enjambment, the opposite of end-stopping, F. W. Dobbs-Allsopp holds, "the linked continuation of phrase or clause across the line boundary creates a certain 'tugging' effect."[1] It is the counterpointing of syntax against the scansion, which creates the sense of "tugging" (and other effects).

However, the concept of vertical grammar and the phenomenon of enjambment are not the same, although they overlap. For one thing, enjambment emphasizes the tugging effect over the line boundary: "In poetry, the role of enjambment is normally to let an idea carry on beyond the restrictions of a single line. Another purpose of enjambment is to

---

1. Dobbs-Allsopp, *On Biblical Poetry*, 45. Like musical counterpoint, where two melodies are played together without losing their separate identities, syntax and prosody work together but remain separate. The phenomenon of double segmentations can be explained thus.

continue a rhythm that is stronger than a permanent end-stop, wherein complicated ideas are expressed in multiple lines."[2]

An example is in Shakespeare's *The Winter's Tale*.

> I am not prone to weeping, as our sex
> Commonly are; the want of which vain dew
> Perchance shall dry your pities; but I have
> That honorable grief lodged here which burns
> Worse than tears drown....

Thus in enjambment two syntactically contiguous elements are separated by a line boundary: x–a // b–x'.

On the other hand, vertical grammar focuses on the grammatical relationship between two items, a and b, in two different lines. The items a and b keep their syntactical or grammatical dependency even if they are not contiguous. In such cases a and b are not enjambic, for they are not contiguous: thus x–a // x'–b.

For example, two elements a and b of a construct chain (a of b) or hendiadys (a and b) can be split into two different lines and not be contiguous, as in the following:

```
a of b (cstr chain)  ⟶  a // b:     x–a // b–x'  ⟶  x–a // x'–b
a and b (hendiadys)  ⟶  a // b:     x–a // b–x'  ⟶  x–a // x'–b
```

One may note that the grammatical dependency exists between a and b vertically, despite the fact that these two elements are no longer contiguous, just parallel, to each other. In other words, the grammatical relations of a and b as a construct chain (a of b) or a hendiadys (a and b) are kept even after these two elements are separated into two lines.

5.2. *Kî* Clause in the Second Line

5.2.1. *Kî* with Enjambment

It is sometimes said that the phenomenon of enjambment is rare in Biblical Hebrew poetry. However, we do see examples such as the following

---

2. See the entry "Enjambment" at https://literarydevices.net/enjambment/.

cases, where the particle *kî* comes in the middle of the second line of a parallelism, as in Ps 22:31:

yābōʾû wəyaggîdû ṣidqātô
ləʿam nôlād kî ʿāśâ

This verse has been analyzed as a very unbalanced bicolon as follows:

> they shall come and proclaim his righteousness to a people yet unborn, that he has done it. (ESV)

It has also been translated as if it is a tricolon:

> They will proclaim his righteousness,
>   declaring to a people yet unborn:
>   He has done it! (NIV11)

However, as the MT cantillation suggests, this verse is a well-balanced bicolon. One can see here an example of enjambment dividing the predicate "proclaim his righteousness to a people yet unborn" (*wəyaggîdû ṣidqātô ləʿam nôlād*) into two lines. From a different viewpoint, the two halves of the predicate have a vertical grammatical dependency. Moreover, the rest of the second line is a *kî* clause, "for he has done it," which is subordinate to the main clause "they shall come… // …unborn":

> They shall come and proclaim his righteousness
> to a people yet unborn, for he has done it.

Thus these two lines hold two different cased of vertical relationships: (1) the phrase *ləʿam nôlād* ("to a people yet unborn") in the second line vertically modifies the main verb *wəyaggîdû* ("they shall proclaim") in the first line; (2) the subordinate clause *kî ʿāśâ* ("for he has done it") modifies the main clause, which is a compound sentence.

The phenomenon of enjambment where the *kî* clause occurs in the second half of the second line can be also recognized in the following parallelisms.

Ps 49:15
ʾak-ʾĕlōhîm yipdeh napšî
miyyad-šəʾôl kî yiqqāḥēnî

> But God will ransom my soul from the power of Sheol,
>   for he will receive me. (ESV)

The MT scansion supports the following line division:

> But God will ransom my soul
> from the power of Sheol, for he will receive me.

In this example the verbal phrase "ransom my soul from the power of Sheol" (*yipdeh napšî miyyad-šəʾôl*) is divided by enjambment. That is, the first half is placed in the last of the first line and the second half in the beginning of the second line.

5.2.1. *Kî* without Enjambment

The next examples should be taken as bicolons in the light of the MT scansion. Although some translations appear to consider them as examples of enjambment, since the Hebrew text has *waw* at the beginning of the second line, they cannot be.

> Ps 18:17 [18]
> *yaṣṣîlēnî mēʾōyəbî ʿāz*
> *ûmiśśōnəʾay kî-ʾāməṣû mimmennî*

The ESV divides the lines as follows:

> He rescued me from my strong enemy
>   and from those who hated me,
>   for they were too mighty for me. (ESV)

However, following the MT scansion, the lines should be divided as follows:

> He rescued me from my strong enemy,
> that is, from those who hated me, for they were too mighty for me.

The conjunction *waw* at the beginning of the second line functions as an explicative *waw*. The expression "from those who hated me" (*miśśōnəʾay*) is simply a synonymous rephrase of "from the strong enemy" (*mēʾōyəbî ʿāz*).

5. Syntax and Scansion in the Biblical Hebrew Poetry

Ps 25:6
zəkōr-raḥămeykā YHWH waḥăsādeykā
kî mēʿôlām hemmā

Remember your mercy, O Lord, and your steadfast love,
for they have been from of old. (ESV)

The verse is better divided as follows:

zəkōr-raḥămeykā YHWH
waḥăsādeykā kî mēʿôlām hemmā

Remember your mercy, O Lord,
    and your steadfast love, for they have been from of old.

This is an example not of enjambment but of a hendiadys, "your mercy and your steadfast love" (*raḥămeykā waḥăsādeykā*), the elements of which are distributed into two parallel lines.

The next several examples are more complicated cases in terms of grammatical structure, but the parallelism is simple.

Ps 18:19 [20]
wayyôṣîʾēnî lammerḥāb
yəḥalləṣēnî kî ḥāpēṣ bî

He brought me out into a broad place;
    he rescued me, because he delighted in me. (ESV)

In this text, the clause "he rescued me" (*yəḥalləṣēnî*) in the second line is simply a restatement of the first line as a whole.

Ps 22:8 (9)
gōl ʾel-YHWH yəpalləṭēhû
yaṣṣîlēhû kî ḥāpēṣ bô

He trusts in the Lord; let him deliver him;
    let him rescue him, for he delights in him! (ESV)

The parallel structure of this text is A–B // B′–X, where A is the basis for the following request, while X is the reason (*kî*: speaker-oriented particle) why the speakers utter such a request as "let him deliver him" (B) // "let him rescue him" (B′).

> Ps 41:4
> ʾănî-ʾāmartî YHWH ḥonnēnî
> rəpāʾāh napšî kî-ḥāṭāʾtî lāk
>
> As for me, I said, "O LORD, be gracious to me;
>   heal me, for I have sinned against you!" (ESV)

This text is similar to the previous one, A–B // B′–X, with the reason (X) for the request for the Lord ("for": speaker-oriented *kî*) to be gracious to the speaker (B) and heal him (B′).

> Ps 60:2
> hirʿaštâ ʾereṣ pəṣamtāh
> rəpāh šəbāreyhā kî-māṭâ
>
> You have made the land to quake; you have torn it open;
>   repair its breaches, for it totters. (ESV)

The structure here is A–A′ // B–X, where A and A′ are, as above, the basis for the following request and X is the reason why (*kî*: speaker-oriented) the speaker made such a request.

In the following examples, the sentences before the *kî*-clause in the second line constitute complex sentences.

> Ps 141:6
> nišməṭû bîdê-selaʿ šōpəṭêhem
> wəšāməʿû ʾămāray kî nāʿēmû
>
> When their judges are thrown over the cliff,
>   then they shall hear my words, for they are pleasant. (ESV)

> Ps 132:14
> zōʾt-mənûḥātî ʿădê-ʿad
> pōh-ʾēšēb kî ʾiwwîtîhā

Since this is my resting place forever,
here I will dwell, for I have desired it.

5.3. *Kî* Clause in the Third Line

We sometimes see such *kî* clauses in the middle of the third line of a tricolon, as in Ps 18:7:

wattigʿaš wattirʿaš hāʾāreṣ
ûmôsədê hārîm yirgāzû
wayyitgāʿăšû kî-ḥārâ lô

Then the earth reeled and rocked;
the foundations also of the mountains trembled
and quaked, because he was angry. (ESV)

This verse is certainly a tricolon, as the MT scansion suggests. No one would object to taking the first two lines as a balanced bicolon with a chiasmus of VP (*wattigʿaš wattirʿaš*)–S (f. sg.: *hāʾāreṣ*) // conj-S (m. pl.: *môsədê hārîm*)–VP (*yirgāzû*). Semantically, however, the first term *wayyitgāʿăšû* in the third line is to be connected with the verb *yirgāzû* in the second line, thus "trembled and quaked." In other words, the division of the verbal phrase "trembled and quaked" (*yirgāzû wayyitgāʿăšû*), both verbs in the third masculine plural form, occurs between the second and third lines. The subordinate clause *kî-ḥārâ lô* ("because he was angry") in the third line modifies the preceding compound sentence vertically.

Thus enjambment can occur in a sentence with *kî*, though not directly before it; still, it is quite rare in the Hebrew tradition of poetic parallelism.

6
Janus Parallelism: Wordplay and Verticality

In this chapter we will deal with a special case of verticality in tricolons, what Cyrus H. Gordon called Janus parallelism, a sophisticated technique of combining a wordplay and parallelism. In 1978 Gordon discussed a tricolon in which an item in the second line has two meanings: one meaning corresponds to a word in the first line, while with other meaning corresponds to a word in the third line.[1] He coined the term *Janus parallelism* for this, after the god Janus, who has two faces looking in opposite directions.

This refers to a semantic aspect of parallelism. Nevertheless, the tricolon as a whole, with a play on word(s) in the middle line, is vertically cohesive as there is often a grammatical relation between both the first and the second lines and the second and the third lines vertically. One such example of Janus parallelism is Song 2:12:[2]

hanniṣṣānîm nirʾû bāʾāreṣ
ʿēt hazzāmîr higgîaʿ
wəqôl hattôr nišmaʿ bəʾarṣēnû

The flowers appear on the earth,
    the time of pruning [or *singing*] has come,
and the voice of the turtledove is heard in our land. (cf. ESV)

In this verse the term *hazzāmîr* is a double entendre, having two meanings: "pruning" and "singing." The meaning "pruning" is in parallel

---

1. Cyrus H. Gordon, "New Directions," *BASP* 15 (1978): 59–60.
2. Cf. Gene M. Schramm ("Poetic Patterning in Biblical Hebrew," in *Michigan Oriental Studies in Honor of George C. Cameron*, ed. Louis L. Orlin [Ann Arbor: University of Michigan, 1976], 179), who notes Song 2:12 as an example of "false syllogism" in "Parallelism of Ambiguity."

with *hanniṣṣānîm* "the flowers" in the first line, while the meaning "singing" parallels *qôl hattôr* "the voice of the turtledove" in the third line. Following Gordon, scholars have found various other examples of this type of parallelism.³

In addition to showing Janus parallelism, in this tricolon the first line and the second lines have a vertical grammatical relation to each other:

A↓   The flowers appear on the earth,
B↑/ X   the time of *pruning/singing* has come,
X'   and the voice of the turtledove is heard in our land.

Not only does the term *hazzāmîr* have a double meaning in this tricolon; the middle line as a whole holds a dual function. It depends grammatically on the first line (A↓ // B↑); that is, "*since* the flowers appear on the earth, the time of pruning has come." On the other hand, the second line (X) is restated in the third line (X') in a different phraseology as "*namely*, the voice of the turtledove is heard in our land."

Other verses show a similar use of Janus parallelism and a vertical grammatical relation.

Gen 49:26

Following in Gordon's steps, Gary Rendsburg discussed the literary phenomenon of Janus parallelism in Gen 49:26.⁴ The MT has been analyzed as follows:

birkōt ʾābîkā
gābərû ʿal-birkōt hôray
ʿad-taʾăwat gibʿōt ʿôlām

---

3. Gary Rendsburg, "Janus Parallelism in Gen 49:26," *JBL* 99 (1980): 291–93; David Toshio Tsumura, "Janus Parallelism in Nah 1:8," *JBL* 102 (1983), 109–11. See also Watson, *Classical Hebrew Poetry*, 159; Anthony R. Ceresko, "Janus Parallelism in Amos's 'Oracles against the Nations' (Amos 1:3–2:16)," *JBL* 113 (1994): 485–90; Scott B. Noegel, *Janus Parallelism in the Book of Job*, JSOTSSup 223 (Sheffield: Sheffield Academic, 1996); John S. Kselman, "Janus Parallelism in Psalm 75:2," *JBL* 121 (2002): 531–32.

4. Rendsburg, "Janus Parallelism in Gen 49:26," 292 n. 4. Note also the spelling ישופטני (1QS X, 13), which is to be vocalized יְשָׁפְטֵנִי. See Gordon, *Ugaritic Textbook*, 68.

6. Janus Parallelism: Wordplay and Verticality

It is usually translated as in the ESV:

The blessings of your father
are mighty beyond the blessings of my parents,
up to the bounties of the everlasting hills.

An ESV note cites the LXX for comparison and explains that "a slight emendation yields":

the blessings of the eternal mountains,
the bounties of the everlasting hills

However, the Hebrew text might be better analyzed as follows:

birkōt ʾābîkā gābərû
ʿal-birkōt hārê ʿad-
taʾăwat gibʿōt ʿôlām

A↓   The blessings of your father are mighty
B↑/X   beyond the blessings of *my parents/the eternal mountains*,
X'   the bounties of the everlasting hills.

The third word of the middle line הוֹרַי *hwry* may be read either *hôray* or *hārê*, for the *mater lectionis* ו (*w*) of הורי (*hwry*) can sometimes represent *qamets* in Biblical Hebrew, as in הֹלֵךְ (Josh 6:13), גֹּלָן (Josh 20:8; 21:27), and the like. Hence the term may mean either "my parents" or "the mountains of." If we take ʿ*ad* as meaning "eternity" rather than "up to" and move it to the end of the second line, the phrase *hārê ʿad* can be taken as "the mountains of eternity," that is, "the eternal mountain," which is a good parallel to "the everlasting hills" as in LXX. So, as Rendburg points out, the form הוֹרַי is a wordplay built into a three-line parallelism, namely, a Janus parallelism. Such a phenomenon can also be recognized in other various places in the Hebrew Bible.

Here again, not only is a particular term or terms in the middle line a double entendre, but the middle line of this tricolon, with "my parents," holds a grammatical dependency vertically with the first line, with "your father" (A↓ // B↑). On the other hand, the phrase "the bounties of the everlasting hills" in the third line is simply a restatement of the phrase "the blessings of the eternal mountains."

Nah 1:8

ûbšeṭep ʿōbēr
kālāh yaʿăśeh מקומה
wəʾōyəbāyw yəraddep-ḥōšek

A↓   But with an overflowing flood
B↑/X   he will completely destroy *her place/his rebels*
X'   and will pursue his enemies into darkness.

The plain meaning of *məqômâ* is "its [= her] place," and it is usually supposed from the context to refer to Nineveh.[5] However, since no mention of Nineveh is made in the poetic portion itself, the suffix "her" has been thought to be "without any antecedent."[6] A majority of scholars therefore, following the LXX, emend the text to *bəqāmāyw*" in his adversaries."[7] This may well be supported by the formulaic use of a word pair *ib* "foe" and *qm* "attacker" common to Ugaritic and Hebrew.[8]

Nevertheless, the MT as it stands does make sense. Although the suffix "her" does not refer directly to Nineveh (1:1), it can point to an understood city, *ʿîr*, a feminine noun, as in Hab 1:10, where "the feminine suffix ... refers *ad sensum* to the idea of a city."[9] Moreover, *mqwmh* is here the object of the verbal phrase, *ʿśh* + *kālâ* "to make a complete destruction" or "completely destroy" (transitive).[10] Thus, 1:8a (A) and 8b (B) grammatically depend on

---

5. Note a recent translation: "he will make an end of Nineveh" (NIV). Cf. Carl Friedrich Keil and Franz Delitzsch, *The Twelve Minor Prophets*, trans. James Martin, 2 vols. (repr., Grand Rapids: Eerdmans, 1970), 2:12.

6. John Merlin Powis Smith, William Hayes Ward, and Julius A. Bewer, *Micah, Zephaniah, Nahum, Habakkuk, Obadiah and Joel*, ICC (Edinburgh: T&T Clark, 1911), 292.

7. BHS; Smith, Ward, and Bewer, *Micah, Zephaniah, Nahum*, 300; Dahood, "Ugaritic-Hebrew Parallel Pairs," 98. See also RSV, NEB, and JB. However, as Godfrey Rolles Driver ("Studies in the Vocabulary of the Old Testament. VIII," *JTS* 36 [1935]: 301) correctly observes, LXX's rendering does not necessarily imply that the Hebrew original was in plural form.

8. See Dahood, "Ugaritic-Hebrew Parallel Pairs," 98; Stanley Gevirtz, "The Ugaritic Parallel to Jeremiah 8:23," *JNES* 20 (1961): 44: "Nah 1:8 (cf. LXX)."

9. Keil and Delitzsch, *The Twelve Minor Prophets*, 2:62.

10. For other examples of two "accusatives" with עשה, see GKC §117ii. Note that the verbal phrase (V-O) functions as a transitive verb that takes another object.

6. Janus Parallelism: Wordplay and Verticality

each other vertically (A↓ // B↑) and describe Yahweh's use of "the overflowing flood" as the agent for destroying the city.

On the other hand, 1:8b and 8c seem to be a synonymous parallelism. Without altering the consonantal spelling, I would like to establish the synonymous relationship between מקומה and אֹיְבָיו. First, the *mater lectionis* ו here also represents *qamets* in Biblical Hebrew. Hence the grapheme מקומה can be vocalized either מְקוֹמָה or מְקוֹמָה. Since the phonetic quality of *qamets* was presumably an open *o*,[11] the pronunciation of the two words differs only in the vowel quality of the second syllable. Second, as illustrated by the fact that the two voiced bilabial consonants *m* and *b* are often interchangeable in Hebrew spellings,[12] the pronunciation of מְקוֹמָה would be close enough to בְקָמָה to be a pun. Third, the verbal idiom *ʿśh* + *kālâ* can appear with or without the preposition ב before its object.[13] Hence in the case of the parallelism of 1:8a and 8b, it appears without ב, while in the synonymous parallelism of 8b and 8c it takes the preposition ב, implied by the spelling מ, before the object קוֹמָה, which is in parallel with אֹיְבָיו. Finally, קוֹמָה, like אֹיֶבֶת and יֹשֶׁבֶת, is probably the feminine abstract noun (participle) "opposition"[14] or "rebellion," which experienced a secondary semantic development to mean "opposer(s)" or "rebel(s)" in a collective sense.[15] This may be supported by the frequent occurrence of a parallelism of an abstract noun with a concrete one, such as צרה and איב.[16]

---

11. See Thomas O. Lambdin, *Introduction to Biblical Hebrew* (New York: Scribners, 1971), xvii.

12. E.g., אבנה (*ketiv*) and אמנה (*qere*) in 2 Kgs 5:12; דימון (MT) and דיבון (1QIsa) in Isa 15:9. See Smith, Ward, and Bewer, *Micah, Zephaniah, Nahum*, 300–301.

13. With ב, see Jer 30:11; 46:28; without ב, see Jer 30:11; 46:28; Ezek 11:13; 20:17; Neh 9:31.

14. Driver ("Studies in the Vocabulary," 301) proposed a "simple alteration" of מְקוֹמָה into מְקוֹמָה and translates the verse: "he will make an end of opposition and will pursue his enemies into darkness." In note 1 Driver refers to Arabic *qwmh* "revolt," *mq'm* "combat," and *mq'wmh* "resistance" as supporting evidence for מְקוֹמָה meaning "opposition." However, if it is not certain whether the masculine noun *mq'm* has the meaning of "combat" as well as the usual sense "a (standing-)place." On the other hand, the first word *qwmh*, being a verbal noun (feminine singular), seems to support my proposal that קָמָה means "opposition" or "rebellion," rather than Driver's.

15. See Diethelm Michel, *Grundlegung einer hebräischen Syntax*, 2 vols. (Neukirchen-Vluyn: Neukirchener Verlag, 1977), 1:71.

16. See Dahood and Penar, "The Grammar of the Psalter," 411.

Thus the spelling מקומה points to two entirely different meanings: "its place" and "(in) the rebel(s)" (B). In the former sense it is closely connected vertical grammatically with 8a (A) in a parallelism; in the latter sense (X) it is synonymously parallel to "his enemies" (X') in 8c.[17] Thus the literary phenomenon of Janus parallelism" in the Hebrew consonantal spelling of Nah 1:8 is another example of sophisticated Hebrew poetic artistry.[18]

While the above Janus parallelisms involve homonymy between the two words such as *zāmîr* "singing" and *zāmîr* "pruning" or similar sound between two completely distinct grammatical terms, polysemy of a single word can also be built in into a Janus parallelism. The next two examples are such cases.

Hab 3:4

wənōgah kā'ôr tihyeh
qarnayim miyyādô lô
wəšām ḥebyôn ʿuzzōh

The brightness shall be as the light;
he has *rays/horns* from his hand,
where his power is hidden.[19]

Habakkuk 3:4 is a long-standing *crux interpretatum* of the Hebrew Bible. In fact, Theodore Hiebert, who made a detailed study of Hab 3, leaves the second line untranslated as "Horns…," while emending the first and the third lines drastically. He further restructures the MT's tricolon and understands the first line (or colon) of verse 4 as the conclusion of the preceding tricolon.[20] On the other hand, J. J. M. Roberts keeps the MT "without radical emendation."[21] When so many hypothetical readings of the "original"

---

17. Note that 8b and 8c are a chiasmus.
18. The LXX, being a translation, could hand down only one of the two meanings of the pun implied by the consonantal text, while the MT vocalization and the Symmachus version preserved the other meaning. See the Japanese poetic device *kakekotoba* in the *tanka* for a similar phenomenon. See Robert H. Brower and Earl Miner, *Japanese Court Poetry* (Stanford, CA: Stanford University Press, 1961).
19. David Toshio Tsumura, "Janus Parallelism in Hab. iii 4," *VT* 54 (2004): 124–28.
20. Theodore Hiebert, *God of My Victory: The Ancient Hymn in Habakkuk 3*, HSM 38 (Atlanta: Scholars Press, 1986), 4, 17–19.
21. Roberts, *Nahum, Habakkuk, and Zephaniah*, 152.

text are proposed and yet no conclusive solution has been reached, it is certainly wise to have a closer look at the available data, in our case, the MT as it stands,[22] by observing the basic structure of language, especially, in the case of poetry, by noting the vertical grammar of parallelism.

Apart from the textual and linguistic problems, there have been opposing views with regard to the literary imagery behind the text. While Roberts sees in this verse storm-god imagery and interprets the term *qarnayim* as representing "two prongs" like the ones extending from the hand of a storm god of Syria-Palestine,[23] Nili Shupak reaffirms the solar connection and interprets *qarnayim* as referring to "rays" of God. She even argues that this text is "a literal description" of the symbol of the Egyptian sun god from the Amarna period.[24] The issue hinges on the meaning of the term *qarnayim* and its position in the poetic structure of verse 4.

Let us begin by considering several modern translations:

His splendor was like the sunrise;
rays flashed from his hand,
where his power was hidden. (NIV)

It is a brilliant light
Which gives off rays on every side—
And therein His glory is enveloped. (JPS)

The brightness was like the sun;
rays came forth from his hand,
where his power lay hidden. (NRSV)

His brightness is like the dawn,
rays of light flash from his hand,
and thereby his might is veiled. (REB)

---

22. For example, the MT *'uppalâ* of Hab 2:4a has been emended in nearly twenty different ways. But one might come closer to a real solution by taking the MT as it stands in the light of new understandings of Hebrew parallelism; see David Toshio Tsumura, "An Exegetical Consideration on Hab 2:4a" [Japanese] *Tojo* 15 (1985): 1–26; see English abstract in *OTA* 9 (1986): 201.

23. Roberts, *Nahum, Habakkuk, and Zephaniah*, 153.

24. Nili Shupak, "The God from Teman and the Egyptian Sun God: A Reconsideration of Habakkuk 3:3–7," *JANES* 28 (2001): 97–116.

The term *qarnayim* has been translated as "rays" in major recent English translations, but the term literally means "horns" (so KJV) and is often used as the symbol of power, for horns are commonly associated with gods and kings in art and literature.[25] The term with this meaning in the second line certainly fits in contextually in parallel with the term ʿzh "his power" in the third line. In fact, *qrn* "horn" and ʿz "power" appear as a word pair in 1 Sam 2:10 and Ps 89:17. As Robert D. Haak notes, the Ugaritic phrase *qrn . dbatk* "the horns of thy *strength*"[26] in *KTU* 1.10.ii.21–22 might add evidence to support "the close association of 'horn' and 'power'" in this passage.[27]

On the other hand, the term has been taken as "rays" in the light of *qrn* "to shine" in Exod 34:29–35 as well as of the rays issuing from the body of solar deities.[28] Shupak, who sees here the symbolism of the Egyptian sun god from the Amarna period, interprets the second line as having the meaning of "God's rays are his hands."[29] However, as Francis I. Andersen warns us, "Poetic comparison of God with the sun is a literary resource, a commonplace, but it is going too far to find behind such language either an original hymn to the sun transferred to Yahweh or traces of an ancient identity of Yahweh and the sun god."[30]

The scholarly world is thus divided between the view that takes *qarnayim* as "horns" and that which takes it as "rays" and whether it is a storm-god image or a solar-god image. However, the close connection between "horns" and "rays" has been noted in the description of the new moon as "horned" in Mesopotamia and Ugarit.[31] Also, in an Eblaite incantation text the phrases "the tail of the sun" and "the two horns of San-Ugaru (= Moon-of-the-Field)" appear. In this context both "the tail" of the sun and the "two horns" of the moon refer to the ray(s) of the sun and of the moon, respectively.[32] However, in these extrabiblical texts the horn is associated with the rays of the moon rather than of the sun.

---

25. See Haak, *Habakkuk*, 86 n. 370.
26. Cyrus H. Gordon, "Poetic Legends and Myths from Ugarit," *Berytus* 25 (1977): 120.
27. Haak, *Habakkuk*, 87.
28. Haak, *Habakkuk*, 86 n. 373.
29. Shupak, "The God from Teman," 105–6.
30. Francis I. Andersen, *Habakkuk: A New Translation with Introduction and Commentary*, AB 25 (Garden City, NY: Doubleday, 2001), 298.
31. Haak, *Habakkuk*, 88 n. 386. For the horns of the moon, see *CAD* 13:137. See also Gordon, *Ugaritic Textbook*, §19.2279.
32. Cyrus H. Gordon, "The Ebla Exorcisms," *Eblaitica* 3 (1992): 136–37.

However, we do have cases where "horn(s)" is associated with the rays or brilliance of the sun. For example, the horns of the crown of Enlil, who is like a wild ox, are said to "shine like the brilliance of the sun" (*kīma šarūr šamši ittananbiṭu*).³³ The association of "horn" and "ray" is in fact made possible in Sumerian by the sign SI, which is sometimes identified with Akkadian *qarnu* ("horn") and sometimes with Akkadian *šarūru* ("radiance, brilliance, sunlight").³⁴ As Andersen notes, "if the sun of the first five colons [3:3–4a] supplies the picture, the "rays" could be the beams of light that come from the upper arms of the sun god in some cylinder seals—stretching the meaning of *yad* a little."³⁵

In the light of the above, I would like to suggest a new solution for this *crux interpretatum*. Alhough Gordon accepted my oral suggestion in his 1986 article,³⁶ it has not been noticed by biblical scholars. Here I would like to present a more detailed discussion of this verse.

Instead of taking *qarnayim* as meaning only "horns," like Albright, Hiebert,³⁷ and Haak, symbolizing power, or only "rays" in association with a solar image like many modern translations and Shupak, I see here a play on words in which both meanings are involved. David W. Baker has also noticed the possibility of "a deliberate play on these two meanings, tying in the brilliance of God's coming with his mighty power which is yet to be detailed,"³⁸ but he did not discuss it further. I would like to explain the entire tricolon as an example of Janus parallelism in which the term *qarnayim* corresponds to "brightness" (*nōgah*) in the first line with the meaning of "rays" and to "his power" (*ʿuzzōh*) in the third line with the meaning of "horns." Thus, my proposed translation would be:

X   The brightness shall be as the light;
X′/A↓   he has *rays/horns* from his hand,
B↑   where his power is hidden.

---

33. BA 10/1 83 no. 9:14–15, cited in *CAD* 17.2:141, 13:139.
34. *CAD* 17.2:141.
35. Andersen, *Habakkuk*, 298. See, for example, Dominique Collon, *First Impressions: Cylinder Seals in the Ancient Near East* (London: British Museum Publications, 1987), 167.
36. Cyrus H. Gordon, "Ḥby, Possessor of Horns and Tail," *UF* 18 (1986): 131.
37. Hiebert, *God of My Victory*, 18.
38. David W. Baker, *Nahum, Habakkuk, Zephaniah: An Introduction and Commentary*, TOTC (Leicester: Inter-Varsity Press, 1988), 71.

In this tricolon the relationship between the first line (X) and the second (X′) seems synonymous with the meaning "rays," while the relationship between the second line with the meaning of "horns" (A) and the third line (B) are grammatically dependent.

Hab 1:9

kullōh ləḥāmās yābôʾ
məgammat pənêhem qādîmâ
wayyeʾĕsōp kaḥôl šebî

All of them come for violence;
they all face forward/like-an-east-wind;
they gather captives like sand.

This verse is generally regarded as unintelligible, but let us see if the above MT scansion as a tricolon with three "accents" in each line makes sense. The second colon, which Wellhausen called "so corrupted that emendation was impossible,"[39] has been interpreted in various ways. However, with our present knowledge, it is most natural to take *məgammat* as the construct form of *məgammâ* "totality."[40] The phrase *qādîmâ*, that is, *qādîm* ("front" or "an east wind") with an adverbial suffix *-â*, can mean either "forward"[41] (JPS, NRSV) or "like an east wind" (REB), hence "like a desert wind" (NIV).

This colon means either "the totality of their faces is forward" or "the totality of their faces is like an east wind." I propose that the entire tricolon is a Janus parallelism in which *qādîmâ* in the second colon has two meanings: "forward" and "like an east wind." With the first meaning the second colon is parallel to the first colon, while with the second meaning it is parallel to the third colon. This produces the following translation:

---

39. See Andersen, *Habakkuk*, 155.
40. *HALOT*, 545.
41. In Ugaritic poetic texts, a term with an adverbial suffix *-h* or an enclitic *-m* is sometimes parallel to a prepositional phrase: for example, *amt-h // ʿd . ṯkm* (*KTU* 1.14.iii.53–54), *krpn-m // b-ks* (1.4.iii.43–44, vi.58–59, 1.5.iv.15–16) and *b-ydk // bm . ymn // klatn-m* (1.14.ii.13–14).

A↓	All of them come for violence,
B↑/X	they all face *forward/like an east wind*;
X'	they gather captives like sand.

Grammatically, the second line is vertically dependent (B↑) on the first line (A↓), explaining how they come "for violence," while the second line with the meaning "like an east wind" (X) is rephrased in the third line (X') as "like sand." The metaphor "to gather like sand" here refers not only to the vast number of the captives (see Hos 2:1) but to the destructiveness of a sandstorm caused by the hot east wind coming from the desert. Hence, "like an east wind" does not imply that the Babylonian army came from the east but that they came destructively like the *hamshin*, the hot wind from the desert in the east.

This way of analyzing the structure of v. 9 seems to be supported also by the grammatical characteristics of the tricolon:

9a: a verbal clause (*yābô'*)	A
9b: a verbless clause	B
9c: a verbal clause (*wayye'ĕsōp*)	A

The verbal expression "come and gather" (*yābô'* ... *wayye'ĕsōp*) describes the sequential actions of the Babylonian army, though the verbal forms (impf. ... waw cons.+ impf.; also in, e.g., 1:10; 2:5; Pss 3:4; 29:9; 49:14) do not match those in the ordinary sequence of classical Hebrew prose.

Thus in the literary device of Janus parallelism the phenomenon of parallelism and a wordplay are combined and well-integrated as another aspect of verticality in the Hebrew poetic parallelism. In fact, the middle line of these tricolons functions as a hinge that connects the first line and the third line in intricate ways. One must dig deeply into this artistic literary expression of poetic parallelism in order to appreciate the sophisticated and beautiful techniques of poetry.[42]

---

42. For a detailed discussion, see Tsumura, "Polysemy and Parallelism," 194–203.

7
Verticality in Hebrew Narrative Prose

The vertical grammar of parallelism can also be seen in highly poetic prose texts. This chapter will examine select examples of this phenomenon.

1 Sam 28:19

wəyittēn YHWH gam ʾet-Yiśrāʾēl ʿimməkā bəyad-Pəlištîm	A
ûmāḥār ʾattāh ûbānêkā ʿimmî	X
gam ʾet-maḥănēh Yiśrāʾēl yittēn YHWH bəyad-Pəlištîm	B

So that the Lord might give even Israel (who is) with you into the hand of Philistines
— tomorrow you and your sons shall be with me—
(so that) even the camp of Israel the Lord might give into the hand of Philistines!

Based on the standard Hebrew prose grammar, McCarter thinks that the text is "corrupt in all witnesses, conflating two versions of one clause."[1] However, it can probably be taken as a tricolon, a three-line parallelism in which the first and the third lines are in chiastic parallelism: a–b–c // b′–a–c.

While the phrases *yittēn YHWH* "the Lord might give" (a) and *bəyad-Pəlištîm* "into the hand of Philistines" (c) are identical in both lines, the third element is repeated with a slight variation "even Israel (who is) with you" // "even the camp of Israel" (b // b′). The second line constitutes the X-line of the A//X//B pattern. In direct speech, prose is often highly poeti-

---

1. P. Kyle McCarter Jr., *I Samuel: A New Translation with Introduction, Notes, and Commentary*, AB 8 (Garden City, NY: Doubleday, 1980), 419.

cal and repetitive, and hence a text such as this should be kept as it stands without emendation.[2]

1 Sam 12:17b[3]

ûd(ə)ʿû ûr(ə)ʾû
kî-rāʿatkem rabbâ
ʾăšer ʿăśîtem bəʿênê YHWH
lišʾôl lākem melek

And know and see
   that the evil that you have done
      by asking for a king for yourselves
   is great in the LORD's eyes.

The syntax of *kî-rāʿatkem rabbâ ʾăšer ʿăśîtem bəʿênê YHWH lišʾôl lākem melek* (lit. "that your evil is great that you have done in the LORD's eyes in asking for a king for yourselves") is somewhat awkward. Conseqently, various suggestions have been made, such as "that your wickedness is great, which you have done in the sight of the LORD, in asking for yourselves a king" (RSV); "that the wickedness that you have done in the sight of the LORD is great in demanding a king for yourselves" (NRSV); "how wicked it was in the LORD's eyes for you to ask for a king" (NEB); and "how displeasing it was to the Lord for you to ask for a king" (REB).

Since the phrase "in the sight of the LORD" normally occurs in the context of moral judgment,[4] it is best to take that phrase as belonging to the main clause ("your evil is great") rather than to the relative clause ("that you have done"); hence McCarter's translation, "that the evil you have done in requesting a king for yourselves is great in Yahweh's eyes," makes good sense.[5] The final phrase "by asking for a king for yourselves"

---

2. Tsumura, "Coordination Interrupted," 126–27.

3. Similarly but not in exactly the same way, Revell sees here an envelope structure, ABBA, which is our AXX'A'. See E. J. Revell, "The Repetition of Introductions to Speech as a Feature of Biblical Hebrew," *VT* 47 (1997): 94 n. 7.

4. See the use of the phrase alongside, e.g., *ṭôb* "good" (Num 24:1), *raʿ* "wicked" Gen 38:7) and *yāšār* "right" (Deut 12:25).

5. McCarter, *I Samuel*, 209.

(*lišʾōl lākem melek*) is thus to be understood as modifying the verb *ʿăśîtem* ("you have done") of the relative clause.

Therefore, it is reasonable to explain that the main clause consists of two phrases—

(a) The evil is great (b) in the sight of the Lord,

—and a relative clause (modifying "evil") consisting of two phrases:

(x) which [evil] you have done (y) by asking for a king for yourselves.

Thus the entire sentence can be divided into two lines that constitute the a–x // b–y pattern.

kî-rāʿatkem rabbâ
   ʾăšer ʿăśîtem
bəʿênê YHWH
   lišʾōl lākem melek

The evil is great (a)
   that you have done (x)
in the sight of the Lord (b)
   by asking for a king for yourselves (y).

Note that verse 19 ("for we have added to all our sins this evil, *by asking for a king for* us") also supports this syntactical understanding, namely, "to add another evil" by asking for a king for us.

The pattern a–x // x′–b can be attested in prose narrative such as 1 Sam 2:14:

kākâ yaʿăśû ləkol-yiśrāʾēl
habbāʾîm šām bəšīlōh

   Such was done to all Israel,
   to those who came there, at Shiloh.

According to normal prose grammar, the phrase "at Shiloh" is to be understood as modifying "those who came" *habbāʾîm* (so REB, NIV). McCarter, holding *šām* ("there") to be unlikely before *bəšīlōh* ("at Shiloh"), emends *šām* to *lzbḥ lyhwh* "to sacrifice to Yahweh" in the light of LXX.⁶ This seems reasonable if the text is taken as straight prose. However, the MT as it stands is better explained if we take verse 14 as constituting a bicolon.

    kākâ yaʿăśû ləkol-yiśrāʾēl
    habbāʾîm šām bəšīlōh

    Such was done, to all Israel,
    those who came there, at Shiloh.

In this bicolon the basic meaning is: "Such was done at Shiloh to all Israel, that is, to those who came there." Thus the prepositional phrase "at Shiloh" (b) in the second line modifies the verb *yaʿăśû* "was done" (lit. "they do") (a) (so NRSV, NASB, JPS) in the first line *vertically*, not the preceding verbal phrase "those who came" *horizontally*. On the other hand, *ləkol-yiśrāʾēl* "to all Israel" (x) is restated as "those who came there" (x′) in the second line. Such parallelism might be explained, like Ps 24:6 (see above), as a–x // x′–b.

1 Sam 16:18

hinnēh rāʾîtî bēn ləyišay bêt hallaḥmî	6 (13)
yōdēaʿ naggēn wəgibbôr ḥayil wəʾîš milḥāmāh	6 (13)
ûnəbôn dābār wəʾîš tōʾar waYHWH ʿimmô	6 (13)

    I have found a son of Jesse the Bethlehemite,
    skillful in playing, who is⁷ a powerful man and a man of war,
    and prudent in speech and handsome, for the LORD is with him!

Here Saul's servant reports to Saul that he found a young man who can help Saul calm down his spirit by music. David is a man of outstanding abilities. However, as he is a youth, the two phrases ("a powerful man" and "a man of war") may refer to David's family background rather than to his own ability ("skillful in playing") and personality ("prudent in speech

---

    6. McCarter, *I Samuel*, 79.
    7. The Hebrew term here is the explicative *waw*.

and handsome"). That is, he is a son of Jesse, the Bethlehemite, a member of the ruling class and a trained fighter. The information that David was a skillful lyre-player was the primary information necessary to Saul in the present context; all the other items were additional. It may be that the servant assumed David to be "a powerful man, a man of war," since he was a son of a well-to-do person whose sons actually engaged in wars (see 1 Sam 17:12–13), but it is more likely that he is referring to Jesse.

The latter possibility is supported by the fact that his utterance has a poetic structure, a tricolon of sorts of 6–6–6 or (13)–(13)–(13). I suggest that it is an a–b // x–y pattern in which the phrase "skillful in playing" (x) modifies "a son" (b) in the first line, and the expression "who is a powerful man and a man of war" (y) modifies "Jesse the Bethlehemite" (c). While two elements, b and c, in the first line hold a horizontal syntagmatic relationship, x and y in the second are just juxtaposed, each holding a vertical grammatical relationship to its corresponding element (i.e., b and c) in the first line. The phrase "prudent in speech and handsome" (x') in the third line also modifies "a son" (b). Thus the entire tricolon can be analyzed as a–b–c // x–y // x'–d:

I have found (a) – a son (b) – to Jesse the Bethlehemite (c)
skillful in playing (x) – a powerful man and a man of war (y)
and prudent in speech and handsome (x') – for the LORD is with him (d)

Here, too, a direct speech can be analyzed in terms of vertical grammar.

When we take into consideration that a book such as 1–2 Samuel, as a historical narrative story, is basically an aural text, we can detect more examples of poetic features.[8]

Gen 1:2

Such poetic features are also recognizable in the initial verses in the Genesis creation story.[9]

---

8. See Tsumura, "Poetic Nature of the Hebrew Narrative Prose," 293–304. Poetic features of narrative prose can be seen also in 1 Sam 2:12, 17; 12:17; 17:6; 18:2, 6; 20:13; 2 Sam 3:22; 14:9; and 22:15. For a detailed discussion, see Tsumura, *The First Book of Samuel*.

9. The poetic features of Gen 1 have been the subject of discussion for some decades. For example, Umberto Cassuto (*From Adam to Noah: A Commentary on the*

wəhāʾāreṣ hāyətāh tōhû wābōhû
wəḥōšek ʿal-pənê təhôm
wərûaḥ ʾĕlōhîm məraḥepet ʿal-pənê hammāyim

As for *the earth, it* was desolate and empty;
there was darkness over the surface of (*its*) *deep*,
but the Spirit of God was hovering over its waters.

Most recently Nicolas Wyatt described the significance of the "darkness" (*ḥōšek*) in Gen 1:2 as "the inchoate medium of revelation," based on his analysis of the poetic structure of Gen 1:2 as a tricolon, which according to him constitutes an a–b–c // a′–c′ // a″–d–c″ pattern.[10] On the surface, Wyatt's "poetical analysis" is seemingly correct, since the subjects (a // a′ // a″), that is, "earth" // "darkness" // "Spirit," are all at the head of the lines. Nevertheless, this analysis does not justify our taking the term *ḥōšek* ("darkness") as having a positive divine quality as against a negative "chaotic" situation in the first line.

One should take into consideration that the terms *ʾereṣ* "earth" (a) and *təhôm* "deep" (a′) are a hyponymous word pair, as discussed elsewhere.[11] As with *bird* and *sparrow*, the semantic field of the former encompasses the semantic field of the latter. Also, the term *tōhû* "desolate" (c) is used parallel to the term *ḥōšek* "darkness" (c′) in other several places also,[12] so it is most likely that these two terms constitute a word pair. If these are a word pair here, despite the surface word order the correspondence between the first two lines in the tricolon could be analyzed as a–b–c // c′–a′, with the parallelism as a whole describing the earth negatively, as a desolate and dark place, not yet the earth as we know. The third line references the same

---

First Chapters of Genesis [Jerusalem: Hebrew University Press, 1961]) noted the existence of "verses with poetic rhythm" such as Gen 1:27, as well as many literary-poetic expressions in Genesis. John S. Kselman ("The Recovery of Poetic Fragments from the Pentateuchal Priestly Source," *JBL* 97 [1978]: 161–73) tries to identify "poetic fragments" in Gen 1.

10. Nicolas Wyatt, "The Darkness of Genesis I 2," *VT* 43 (1993): 543–54.

11. For this term, see chapter 2, above; see also Tsumura, "A 'Hyponymous' Word Pair," 258–69; Tsumura, *Creation and Destruction*, 58–63.

12. Isa 45:19; Job 12:24–25; cf. Jer 4:23. See David Toshio Tsumura, *The Earth and the Waters in Genesis 1 and 2: A Linguistic Analysis*, JSOTSup 83 (Sheffield: JSOT Press, 1989), 34–38.

condition, albeit positively:[13] God's Spirit was about to be breathed out as a breath into an utterance.[14] Thus verse 2 as a whole describes the setting for God's first creative action, "And he said,"[15] that is, God's first utterance: "Let the light be!"

2 Sam 7:22

David's prayer in 2 Sam 7:18b-29 is usually treated as a prose prayer, but it is not written in the typical narrative prose style.[16] I suggest that we should treat this prayer as a whole as poetic prose. If so, verse 22 consists of a tetracolon, that is, a four-line parallelism, and can be translated as follows:

ʿal-kēn gādaltā ʾădōnāy YHWH
kî-ʾên kāmôkā
wəʾên ʾĕlōhîm zûlātekā
bəkōl ʾăšer-šāmaʿnû bəʾoznênû

Therefore, I say,[17] you are great, O Lord GOD	A↓
—for there is no one like you,	X
and there is no God besides you—	X′
in all that we heard with our ears.	B↑

The particle ʿal-kēn ("therefore") usually introduces a logical conclusion or consequence: "A, *therefore* B." For example, 2 Sam 7:27:

You have revealed this to your servant, saying
    "A house I will build for you."
Therefore [ʿal-kēn] your servant has found courage
to pray this prayer to you.

---

13. Hence "but" in the beginning of the line.
14. David Toshio Tsumura, "'The Breath of God' (Gen 1:2c) in Creation" [Japanese with English summary], *Exeg* 9 (1998): 21–30.
15. Note that this is the first *wayqtl* (narrative past) form in this story.
16. Moshe Greenberg, *Biblical Prose Prayer: As a Window to the Popular Religion of Ancient Israel* (Berkeley: University of California Press, 1983).
17. For the speaker-oriented functions of the particle ʿal-ken, see my "The Speaker-Oriented Connective Particle," and the discussion in my *The Second Book of Samuel*, NICOT (Grand Rapids: Eerdmans, 2019), 142–46.

In this verse, "therefore" (ʿal-kēn) indicates the result of the first half: the Lord revealed, and therefore David found courage.

However, in 2 Sam 7:22 ʿal-kēn does not indicate the result of the previous sentence: God's promise did not *make* God great; rather, it showed David that God *was* great. In other words, it introduces a sentence on a different level from the preceding discourse in verse 21, giving a comment or explanatory note from the speaker's perspective: "A *therefore I say* B" or "A is why *I say* B" or "because of A, *I say* B." It hints that A is an indirect cause of B, but not a direct cause. Thus it should be translated as follows:

> Therefore, [*I say,*] you are great, O Lord GOD.

This usage is speaker-oriented like *kî*.[18]

The grammatical structure of verse 22, however, is somewhat strange according to the traditional understanding of the prose grammar. A literal translation is:

> Therefore, [*I say,*] you are great [*qtl*], O Lord GOD.
> For there is none like you, and there is no God besides you
> *in* all [*bəkōl*] that we heard with our ears.

The last clause is usually translated as "according to all that we have heard with our ears" (ESV) or "as we have heard with our own ears." (NIV; also JPS, REB) However, it is rather forced to translate the preposition *bə* as "according to" or "as" in this context.

If the entire verse is regarded as a tetracolon, we can see that grammatically the fourth line depends on the first line *vertically*.

> You are great, O Lord GOD,
> in all that we heard with our ears.

Between the two lines, a synonymous bicolon is inserted that gives the reason why David says that God is great: "for[19] there is no one like you, and there is no God besides you." Verse 22 thus constitutes a parallelistic

---

18. See Claasen, "Speaker-Oriented Functions of *ki*," 29–46; Tsumura, *The First Book of Samuel*, 48–49. See also my "Speaker-Oriented Connective Particle."

19. Note that the particle "for" (*kî*) is speaker-oriented.

structure of the AXX'B pattern,[20] or an inserted bicolon, as in Amos 1:5, Pss 9:6, 17:1, and other verses.[21]

Therefore [I say], you are great, O Lord GOD!	A↓
—For there is no one like you;	X
and there is no God besides you—	X'
in all that we heard [about you] with our ears.	B↑

In conclusion, poetic texts and some narrative prose texts in the Bible exhibit parallelism in which correspondence and repetition between two parallel lines are characterized by vertical grammar. To understand these texts correctly one certainly needs to recognize the vertical grammatical relationships in parallelism.

---

20. For Ps 89:36–37 and other passages, see chapter 4, above.
21. See Tsumura, *The First Book of Samuel*, 60–64; also Tsumura, "Vertical Grammar of Biblical Hebrew Parallelism," 447–59.

8
Vertical Grammar of Parallelism in Ugaritic Poetry

Cases of vertical grammar can be recognized also in some Ugaritic poetic texts, though they are harder to find in Ugaritic due to the lack of vowel letters in most of the words. As is the case of Hebrew parallelism, one should carefully distinguish between the phenomena of verbal ellipsis and that of vertical grammar.[1] As in the Hebrew poetic texts, there are more cases of verbal ellipsis in the Ugaritic poetry.

KTU 1.2.i.37–38

> *hw . ybl . argmnk*
> *k ilm / [xxxx] ybl .*
> *k bn . qdš . mnḥyk*

> He will indeed bring you tribute,
> like (one of) the gods [a gift] he will bring [you],
> like (one of) the sons of the Holy One (he will bring) you presents.[2]

Here, as Dennis Pardee holds, the verb ("he will bring") is seemingly ellipsized in the third line.[3]

KTU 1.3.iii.20–22

> *dm . rgm / iṯ . ly . w . argmk*
> *hwt . w . aṯnyk*

---
1. See §3.3, above.
2. Pardee, *The Ugaritic Texts*, 56.
3. Pardee, *The Ugaritic Texts*, 58 n. 35.

For I have something to tell you,
(I have) a matter to recount to you.[4]

KTU 1.2.i.18–19

tn . bʿl[. w ʿnnh]
bn . dgn . arṯm . pḏh

Give (up) *Baʿlu* [and his attendants],
(give up) the Son of Dagan, that I might take possession of his gold.[5]

KTU 1.14.i.33–35

šnt . tluan (tlunn) / w yškb .
nhmmt / w yqmṣ .

Sleep (a) overcomes him (b) and he lies down (c),
slumber (A′) (overcomes him) and he curls up (c′).

The structure of this parallelism is a-b-c // A′-c′. Here the verbal phrase (b) *tluan* (overcomes him) is ellipsized in the second line, as in Ps 18:14 (see §3.3, above); *nhmmt* (A′) is a ballast variant for *šnt* (a) in the first line.

KTU 1.14.i.26–27

This text is definitely a case for vertical grammar rather than verbal ellipsis.

yʿrb . b ḥdrh . ybky
b ṯn . ʿ(R:p)gmm . w ydmʿ

He enters (a) his room (b), he weeps (x),
while speaking forth (c) (his) grief (d), and he sheds tears (x′).

---

4. Pierre Bordreuil and Dennis Pardee, *A Manual of Ugaritic*, LSAWS 3 (Winona Lake, IN: Eisenbrauns, 2009), 165; see also *COS* 1.86:251.
5. *COS* 1.86.246

He enters his room, he weeps,
as he speaks forth (his) grief, he sheds tears.[6]

According to Nicolas Wyatt, the *waw* in the second line occurs because of "an erroneous transposition."[7] He translates the text as follows:

He went into his chamber (and) wept;
redoubling his lamentations, he sobbed.

However, the text makes good sense as is when we recognize vertical grammar. In this text, the phrase *b ṯn . ʿgmm* (c–d) in the second line is grammatically dependent on the verb *yʿrb* (a) in the first line and thus means: "He enters his room while speaking forth (his) grief." On the other hand, the verbal phrases *ybky* (x), in asyndeton (without a conjuction) and *w ydmʿ* (x′) correspond to each other synonymously: "(and) he weeps and sheds tears." The entire bicolon (a–b–x // c–d–x′) may be paraphrased thus:

He enters his room while speaking forth his grief,
(and) he weeps and sheds tears.

Thus also in Ugaritic poetic texts there exist, albeit in a limited number, examples of the same feature of a vertical grammatical relation between two or more parallel lines that we see in Hebrew poetic texts. Pardee noted my 2009 paper and referred to the feature as the "verticality" of parallelism, a term that I accept wholeheartedly.[8]

As in Hebrew poetic parallelism, such verticality in Ugaritic poetic parallelism can be typically observed in bicolons in which two lines constitute a simple sentence.[9]

KTU 1.3.i.20–22

yšr . ġzr . ṭb . ql
ʿl . bʿl . bṣrt ṣpn

---

6. See Bordreuil and Pardee, *A Manual of Ugaritic*, 170.
7. Nicolas Wyatt, *Religious Texts from Ugarit: The Words of Ilimilku and his Colleagues*, Biblical Seminar 53 (Sheffield: Sheffield Academic, 1998), 183 n. 25.
8. Pardee, *The Ugaritic Texts*, 56–58.
9. Chapters 1 and 4.

The good-voiced youth sings
For Baal in the heights of Ṣapan.[10]

The two lines constitute a phonetic parallelism with the assonance of [r], [l], [b], [ʿ], and [ġ], while grammatically they are a simple sentence.

KTU 1.3.i.18–19

This text is also an example of vertical grammar, since the nucleus of a sentence (S[V_1–V_2–V_3] is in the first line and the modifier in the second line, though the sentence is not a simple sentence.

> qm . ybd . yšr
> mṣltm . bd . nʿm

> He arises, chants, and sings,
> Cymbals (being) in the hands of the goodly one.[11]

The structure of this bicolon (SV_1–V_2–V_3 // M) is a–b–c // d–e–f. None of the words in the first line corresponds semantically to any in the second line, so one might consider the lines as nonparallel. However, phonetically, assonance of [m] suggests a parallelistic structure.[12] The entire bicolon constitutes a complex sentence. It is clear that the second line as a whole holds a grammatical dependence with the first line vertically.

KTU 1.2.iv.15–16, also 13–14, 20–21, 23–24

> yrtqṣ . ṣmd . bd bʿl .
> km . nšr / b uṣbʿth

> The club swoops from the hand of Baal
> Like an eagle from his fingers.[13]

One might take this as an example of verbal ellipsis in the second line,

---

10. Pardee, *Ugaritic and Hebrew Poetic Parallelism*, 2.
11. Pardee, *Ugaritic and Hebrew Poetic Parallelism*, 2.
12. For this phenomenon, see chapter 2.
13. Gordon, "Poetic Legends and Myths from Ugarit," 73.

The club swoops from the hand of Baal;
[it swoops] like an eagle from his fingers.

However, another way of explanation is that the phrase "like an eagle" (b) modifies the verb "to swoop" in the first line vertically, especially since the verb "to swoop" is usually connected with the image of falconry.[14] The prepositional phrase "from his fingers" (x′) is simply a restatement of the phrase "from the hand of Baal" (x). Hence the structure of this bicolon is a–x // b–x′, and the bicolon as a whole can be translated as follows:

The club swoops like an eagle from the hand of Baal,
namely, from his fingers.

KTU 1.18.iv.24–26, 36–37

tṣi . km / rḥ . npš h .
km . iṯl . brlth .
km / qṭr . b aph

Let his soul go out like wind
Like a *gust* his spirit
Like smoke out of his nose![15]

Pardee translates similarly:

So that his life force rushes out like wind,
like spittle his vitality,
like smoke from his nostrils.[16]

The phrase "smoke out of his nostrils" might be taken as an image of the angry person, as suggested by Ps 18:8 (Yahweh's wrath) and Job 41:20 (the smoke out of Leviathan's nostrils). However, here in the Aqhat story, anger does not seem to be involved in the description of the hero's death; it is rather a description of the "departure" of his breath as in Ps 146:4.

---

14. See Jeanny Vorys Canby, "Falconry (Hawking) in Hittite Lands," *JNES* 61 (2002): 161–201.
15. Gordon, "Poetic Legends and Myths from Ugarit," 19.
16. Dennis Pardee, "The ʾAqhatu Legend," *COS* 1.103:350.

In the parallel structure of this tricolon, there are three metaphors, or similes, "like wind" (x), "like spittle" (x'), and "like smoke" (x''), for the hero's "life force" (b) and "vitality" (b'). The phrase "from his nostrils" (c) in the third line is most likely to be taken as an adverbial phrase modifying the verb rushes out (a) in the first line. The grammatical structure can be described as follows: V–M–S // M'–S' // M''–AdvPh. Thus we should recognize here also the phenomenon of vertical grammar over three lines of parallelism.

"rushes out" (a) – "like wind" (x) – "his life force" (b)
"like spittle" (x') – "his vitality" (b')
"like smoke" (x'') – "from his nostrils" (c)

In other words, this tricolon most likely constitutes a simple sentence and should be translated in a prosaic style as follows:

So that his life force, namely, his vitality, rushes out from his nostrils like wind, like spittle, like smoke.

KTU 1.3.iii.28–31

The next example is a tetracolon in which the first line is a sentence nucleus (SVO) and the next three lines are the modifiers.

atm . w ank / ibġyh .
b tk . ġry . il . ṣpn
b qdš . b ġr . nḥlty
b nʿm . b gbʿ . tliyt

Come and I will explain it (to you)
in my mountain, Divine Ṣapunu,
in the holy place, in the mountain that is my personal possession,
in the goodly place, the hill of my victory.[17]

Here we can see a vertical grammatical relationship between the first and second lines:

---

17. Bordreuil and Pardee, *A Manual of Ugaritic*, 165.

Come and I will explain it (to you)
in my mountain, Divine Ṣapunu,

The next two lines, that is, the third and fourth lines, are simply in apposition to the second line. Thus the four-line parallelism as a whole constitutes a simple sentence.

In conclusion, the phenomenon of vertical grammar of parallelism is a characteristic of Ugaritic poetry just as it is of biblical Hebrew poetry. One might surmise that this vertical feature, that is, verticality, was a typical characteristic of the epic literature, for its narrative poetic style urges a vertical continuity in the storytelling with poetic parallelism.

Conclusions

Throughout this work we have seen that *verticality* is one of the characteristics of the grammar of poetic parallelism. While grammatical dependency normally works horizontally in prose, in parallelistic structures, both in poetry and in prose, it works vertically. Theoretically, this principle is a matter-of-course, but in actuality it has not been rightly understood and never investigated concretely by biblical scholars.

In this monograph I have shown not only that poetic lines as a whole are vertically dependent on each other, having verticality between an A and a B line, but also that elements a and b in the corresponding lines hold a vertical grammatical relationship with each other. The phenomenon is well-illustrated by the patterns a–x // b–x′ and A//X//X′//B, in which element a and element b or the A-line and the B-line have a vertical grammatical relationship with each other in parallelism, while element x′ or the X′-line is simply a restatement of element x or the X-line.

In theory and practice, *verticality*, that is, the existence of a vertical relation between two parallel lines, is a characteristic of poetic language, just as *linearity* is a characteristic of prose language. Poetic parallelism well illustrates this dual nature of language, which is caused by the double segmentation of human language. In other words, poetic language is characterized by syntactic segmentation as well as by poetic segmentation. The former results in end-stopping at the close of sentences in prose language, while the latter results in parallel lines by scansion in poetic language. This very nature of poetic language causes us to recognize two types of grammar, horizontal grammar and vertical grammar, the latter of which has been the concern in this monograph.

Bibliography

Alter, Robert. *The Art of Biblical Poetry.* New York: Basic Books, 1985.
Anderson, A. A. *2 Samuel.* WBC 11. Dallas: Word, 1989.
Andersen, Francis I. *Habakkuk: A New Translation with Introduction and Commentary.* AB 25. Garden City, NY: Doubleday, 2001.
Andersen, Francis I., and David Noel Freedman. *Hosea: A New Translation with Introduction and Commentary.* AB 24. Garden City, NY: Doubleday, 1980.
Avishur, Yitshak. *Stylistic Studies of Word-Pairs in Biblical and Ancient Semitic Literatures.* AOAT 210. Neukirchen-Vluyn: Neukirchener Verlag, 1984.
Baker, David W. *Nahum, Habakkuk, Zephaniah: An Introduction and Commentary.* TOTC. Leicester: Inter-Varsity Press, 1988.
Berlin, Adele. *The Dynamics of Biblical Parallelism.* Bloomington: Indiana University Press, 1985. 2nd ed. Grand Rapids: Eerdmans, 2008.
———. "Parallel Word Pairs: A Linguistic Explanation." *UF* 15 (1983): 7–16.
———. "Shared Rhetorical Features in Biblical and Sumerian Literature." *JANES* 10 (1978): 35–42.
Boodberg, Peter A. "Syntactical Metaplasia in Stereoscopic Parallelism." In *Cedules from a Berkeley Workshop on Asiatic Philology* (1954). Repr. as pages 184–85 in *Selected Works of Peter A. Boodberg.* Compiled by Alvin P. Cohen. Berkeley: University of California Press, 1979.
Bordreuil, Pierre, and Dennis Pardee. *A Manual of Ugaritic.* LSAWS 3. Winona Lake, IN: Eisenbrauns, 2009.
Brower, Robert H., and Earl Miner. *Japanese Court Poetry.* Stanford, CA: Stanford University Press, 1961.
Canby, Jeanny Vorys. "Falconry (Hawking) in Hittite Lands." *JNES* 61 (2002): 161–201.
Cassuto, Umberto. *From Adam to Noah: A Commentary on the First Chapters of Genesis.* Jerusalem: Hebrew University Press, 1961.

Caton, Steve C. "Contributions of Roman Jakobson." *Annual Review of Anthropology* 16 (1987): 223–60.

Ceresko, Anthony R. "Janus Parallelism in Amos's 'Oracles against the Nations' (Amos 1:3–2:16)." *JBL* 113 (1994): 485–90.

Chavel, Simeon. "Biblical 'Alternation' and Its Poetics." Pages 179–203 in *"Like 'Ilu Are You Wise": Studies in Northwest Semitic Languages and Literatures in Honor of Dennis G. Pardee*. Edited by H. H. Hardy II, Joseph Lam, and Eric D. Reymond. Chicago: Oriental Institute, 2022.

Claasen, Walter T. "Speaker-Oriented Functions of *kî* in Biblical Hebrew." *JNSL* 11 (1983): 29–46.

Clines, David J. A. "The Parallelism of Greater Precision: Notes from Isaiah 40 for a Theory of Hebrew Poetry." Pages 77–100 in *Directions in Biblical Hebrew Poetry*. Edited by Elaine R. Follis. JSOTSup 40. Sheffield: JSOT Press, 1987.

Collins, Terence. *Line-Forms in Hebrew Poetry: A Grammatical Approach to the Stylistic Study of the Hebrew Prophets*. StPohl 7. Rome: Biblical Institute Press, 1978.

Collon, Dominique. *First Impressions: Cylinder Seals in the Ancient Near East*. London: British Museum Publications, 1987.

Dahood, Mitchell. "A New Metrical Pattern in Biblical Poetry." *CBQ* 29 (1967): 574–79.

———. "Ugaritic-Hebrew Parallel Pairs." Pages 1–33 in vol. 1 of *Ras Shamra Parallels: The Texts from Ugarit and the Hebrew Bible*. Edited by Loren R. Fisher and Stan Rummel. 3 vols. Rome: Pontifical Biblical Institute, 1972–1981.

Dahood, Mitchell, and Tadeusz Penar. "The Grammar of the Psalter." Pages 361–456 in *Psalms III, 101–150: Translated with an Introduction and Notes*, by Mitchell Dahood. AB 17A. Garden City, NY: Doubleday, 1970.

Dobbs-Allsopp, F. W. *On Biblical Poetry*. Oxford: Oxford University Press, 2015.

Driver, Godfrey Rolles. "Studies in the Vocabulary of the Old Testament. VIII." *JTS* 36 (1935): 293-301.

Edelman, Diana Vikander. "The Meaning of *qiṭṭēr*." *VT* 35 (1985): 395–404.

Exum, J. Cheryl. *Song of Songs: A Commentary*. OTL. Louisville: Westminster John Knox, 2005.

Freedman, David Noel. "On the Death of Abner." Pages 125–27 in *Love and Death in the Ancient Near East: Essays in Honor of Marvin H.*

Pope. Edited by John H. Marks and Robert M. Good. Guilford, CT: Four Quarters, 1987.

Garrett, Duane A. *Proverbs, Ecclesiastes, Song of Songs*. NAC. Nashville: Broadman, 1993.

Geller, Stephen A. *Parallelism in Early Biblical Poetry*. HSM 20. Missoula, MT: Scholars Press, 1979.

Gevirtz, Stanley. "The Ugaritic Parallel to Jeremiah 8:23." *JNES* 20 (1961): 41–46.

Gordon, Cyrus H. "The Ebla Exorcisms." *Eblaitica* 3 (1992): 127–38.

———. "Ḥby, Possessor of Horns and Tail." *UF* 18 (1986): 129–32.

———. "New Directions." *BASP* 15 (1978): 59–66.

———. "Poetic Legends and Myths from Ugarit." *Berytus* 25 (1977): 5–133.

———. *Ugaritic Textbook: Grammar, Texts in Transliteration, Cuneiform Selections, Glossary, Indices*. AnOr 38. Rome: Pontifical Biblical Institute, 1965.

Greenberg, Moshe. *Biblical Prose Prayer: As a Window to the Popular Religion of Ancient Israel*. Berkeley: University of California Press, 1983.

Greenstein, Edward L. "Two Variations of Grammatical Parallelism in Canaanite Poetry and Their Psycholinguistic Background." *JANESCU* 6 (1974): 87–105.

Gzella, Holger. "Parallelismus und Asymmetrie in ugaritischen Texten." Pages 133–38 in *Parallelismus membrorum*. Edited by Andreas Wagner. OBO 224. Fribourg: Academic Press; Göttingen: Vandenhoeck & Ruprecht, 2007.

Haak, Robert D. *Habakkuk*. VTSup 44. Leiden: Brill, 1992.

Herbert, Edward D. *Reconstructing Biblical Dead Sea Scrolls: A New Method Applied to the Reconstruction of 4QSam[a]*. Leiden: Brill, 1997.

Hess, Richard S. *Song of Songs*. BCOTWP. Grand Rapids: Baker Academic, 2005.

Hiebert, Theodore. *God of My Victory: The Ancient Hymn in Habakkuk 3*. HSM 38. Atlanta: Scholars Press, 1986.

Jakobson, Roman. "Grammatical Parallelism and Its Russian Facet." *Language* 42 (1966): 399–429.

———. "Linguistics and Poetics." Pages 350–77 in *Style in Language*. Edited by Thomas A. Sebeok. Cambridge: MIT Press, 1960.

Kao, Yu-Kung, and Tsu-Lin Mei. "Meaning, Metaphor, and Allusion in T'ang Poetry." *HJAS* 38 (1978), 281–356.

Keel, Othmar. *The Song of Songs*. CC. Minneapolis: Fortress, 1994.

Keil, Carl Friedrich, and Franz Delitzsch. *The Twelve Minor Prophets.* Translated by James Martin. 2 vols. Repr., Grand Rapids: Eerdmans, 1970.

Kroll, Paul W. Review of *Selected Works of Peter A. Boodberg*, compiled by Alvin P. Cohen. *Chinese Literature: Essays, Articles, Reviews* 2 (1980): 271–73.

Kselman, John S. "Janus Parallelism in Psalm 75:2." *JBL* 121 (2002): 531–32.

———. "The Recovery of Poetic Fragments from the Pentateuchal Priestly Source." *JBL* 97 (1978): 161–73.

Kugel, James L. *The Idea of Biblical Poetry: Parallelism and Its History.* New Haven: Yale University Press, 1981.

Lambdin, Thomas O. *Introduction to Biblical Hebrew.* New York: Scribners, 1971.

Landy, Francis. "In Defense of Jakobson." *JBL* 111 (1992): 105–13.

Liu, David Jason. "Parallel Structures in the Canon of Chinese Poetry: The Shih Ching." *Poetics Today* 4 (1983): 639–53.

Loewenstamm, Samuel E. "The Expanded Colon in Ugaritic and Biblical Verse." *JSS* 14 (1969): 176–96.

———. "The Expanded Colon, Reconsidered." *UF* 7 (1975): 261–64.

Lowth, Robert. *Isaiah: A New Translation with a Preliminary Dissertation and Notes.* London: Tegg, 1848. Orig. 1778.

———. *Lectures on the Sacred Poetry of the Hebrews.* Translated by George Gregory. 3rd ed. London: Tegg & Son, 1835. Translation of *De sacra poesi hebraeorum: Praelectiones academiae Oxonii habitae.* Oxford: Clarendon, 1753.

Lunn, Nicholas P. *Word-Order Variation in Biblical Hebrew Poetry: Differentiating Pragmatics and Poetics.* Milton Keynes: Paternoster, 2006.

Lyons, John. *Introduction to Theoretical Linguistics.* Cambridge: Cambridge University Press, 1968.

———. *Semantics.* 2 vols. Cambridge: Cambridge University Press, 1977.

McCarter, P. Kyle, Jr. *I Samuel: A New Translation with Introduction, Notes, and Commentary.* AB 8. Garden City, NY: Doubleday, 1980.

———. *II Samuel: A New Translation with Introduction, Notes, and Commentary.* AB 9. Garden City, NY: Doubleday, 1984.

Melamed, Ezra Z. "Break-Up of Stereotype Phrases as an Artistic Device in Biblical Poetry." Pages 115–53 in *Studies in the Bible.* Edited by Chaim Rabin. Scripta Hierosolymitana 8. Jerusalem: Magnes, 1961.

Michel, Diethelm. *Grundlegung einer hebräischen Syntax*. 2 vols. Neukirchen-Vluyn: Neukirchener Verlag, 1977.

Miller, Cynthia L. "Ellipsis Involving Negation in Biblical Poetry." Pages 37–52 in *Seeking Out the Wisdom of the Ancients: Essays Offered to Honor Michael V. Fox*. Edited by Ronald L. Troxel, Kelvin G. Friebel and Dennis R. Magary. Winona Lake, IN: Eisenbrauns, 2005.

———. "A Linguistic Approach to Ellipsis in Biblical Poetry (Or, What to Do When Exegesis of What Is There Depends on What Isn't)." *BBR* 13 (2003): 251–70.

Moers, Gerald. "Der Parallelismus (membrorum) als Gegenstand ägyptologischer Forschung." Pages 147–66 in *Parallelismus membrorum*. Edited by Andreas Wagner. OBO 224. Fribourg: Academic Press; Göttingen: Vandenhoeck & Ruprecht, 2007.

Muraoka, Takamitsu. "Between Linguistics and Philology." *ANES* 41 (2004): 87–88.

Murphy, Roland E., and S. Dean McBride Jr. *The Song of Songs: A Commentary on the Book of Canticles or the Song of Songs*. Hermeneia. Minneapolis: Fortress, 1990.

Niccacci, Alviero. "Analysing Biblical Hebrew Poetry." *JSOT* 74 (1997): 77–93.

———. "The Biblical Hebrew Verbal System in Poetry." Pages 247–68 in *Biblical Hebrew in Its Northwest Semitic Setting: Typological and Historical Perspectives*. Edited by Steven E. Fassberg and Avi Hurvitz. Jerusalem: Magnes, 2006.

Noegel, Scott B. *Janus Parallelism in the Book of Job*. JSOTSup 223. Sheffield: Sheffield Academic, 1996.

Notarius, Tania. "'Double Segmentation' in Biblical Hebrew Poetry and the Poetic Cantillation System." *ZDMG* 168 (2018): 333–52.

O'Connor, M. *Hebrew Verse Structure*. Winona Lake, IN: Eisenbrauns, 1980.

Pardee, Dennis. "The 'Aqhatu Legend." *COS* 1.103:343–56.

———. *Ugaritic and Hebrew Poetic Parallelism: A Trial Cut*. VTSup 39. Leiden: Brill, 1988.

———. *The Ugaritic Texts and the Origins of West-Semitic Literary Composition*. Schweich Lectures of the British Academy 2007. Oxford: Oxford University Press, 2012.

Pope, Marvin H. *Song of Songs: A New Translation with Introduction and Commentary*. AB 7C. Garden City, NY: Doubleday, 1977.

Qimron, Elishaʿ. "The Lament of David over Abner." Pages 143–47 in vol. 1 of *Birkat Shalom: Studies in the Bible, Ancient Near Eastern Literature, and Postbiblical Judaism Presented to Shalom M. Paul on the Occasion of His Seventieth Birthday*. Edited by Chaim Cohen et al. 2 vols. Winona Lake, IN: Eisenbrauns, 2008.

Rendsburg, Gary. "Janus Parallelism in Gen 49:26." *JBL* 99 (1980): 291–93.

Revell, E. J. "The Repetition of Introductions to Speech as a Feature of Biblical Hebrew." *VT* 47 (1997): 91–110.

Roberts, J. J. M. *Nahum, Habakkuk, and Zephaniah*. OTL. Louisville: Westminster John Knox, 1991.

Schafer, Edward H., and Alvin P. Cohen. "Peter A. Boodberg, 1903–1972." *JAOS* 94 (1974): 1–13.

Schramm, Gene M. "Poetic Patterning in Biblical Hebrew." Pages 167–91 in *Michigan Oriental Studies in Honor of George C. Cameron*. Edited by Louis L. Orlin. Ann Arbor: University of Michigan, 1976.

Segert, Stanislav. *A Basic Grammar of the Ugaritic Language*. Berkeley: University of California Press, 1984.

———. "Parallelism in Ugaritic Poetry." *JAOS* 103 (1983): 295–306.

Shupak, Nili. "The God from Teman and the Egyptian Sun God: A Reconsideration of Habakkuk 3:3-7." *JANES* 28 (2001): 97–116.

Smith, John Merlin Powis, William Hayes Ward, and Julius A. Bewer. *Micah, Zephaniah, Nahum, Habakkuk, Obadiah and Joel*. ICC. Edinburgh: T&T Clark, 1911.

Stager, Lawrence E. "Key Passages." *Eretz-Israel* 27 (2003): 240*–45*.

Taber, Charles R. "Semantics." *IDB Supplement*, 800–807.

Tsumura, David Toshio. "'The Breath of God' (Gen 1:2c) in Creation" [Japanese with English summary]. *Exeg* 9 (1998): 21-30.

———. "Coordination Interrupted, or Literary Insertion AX&B Pattern, in the Books of Samuel." Pages 117–32 in *Literary Structure and Rhetorical Strategies in the Hebrew Bible*. Edited by Lénart J. de Regt, Jan de Waard, and Jan P. Fokkelman. Assen: Van Gorcum, 1996.

———. *Creation and Destruction: A Reappraisal of the* Chaoskampf *Theory in the Old Testament*. Winona Lake, IN: Eisenbrauns, 2005.

———. *The Earth and the Waters in Genesis 1 and 2: A Linguistic Analysis*. JSOTSup 83. Sheffield: JSOT Press, 1989.

———. "An Exegetical Consideration on Hab 2:4a" [Japanese]. *Tojo* 15 (1985): 1–26. See English abstract in *OTA* 9 (1986): 201.

———. *The First Book of Samuel*. NICOT. Grand Rapids: Eerdmans, 2007.

———. "A 'Hyponymous' Word Pair, *'rṣ* and *thm(t)*, in Hebrew and Ugaritic." *Bib* 69 (1988): 258–69.

———. "'Inserted Bicolon,' the AXYB Pattern, in Amos I 5 and Psalm IX 7." *VT* 38 (1988): 234–36.

———. "Janus Parallelism in Hab. iii 4." *VT* 54 (2004): 124–28.

———. "Janus Parallelism in Nah 1:8." *JBL* 102 (1983): 109–11.

———. "Literary Insertion, AXB Pattern, in Hebrew and Ugaritic: A Problem of Adjacency and Dependency in Poetic Parallelism." *UF* 18 (1986): 351–61.

———. "Literary Insertion (AXB Pattern) in Biblical Hebrew." *VT* 33 (1983): 468–82.

———. "Literary Insertion (AXB) Pattern in Biblical Hebrew." Pages 1–6 in *Proceedings of the Eighth World Congress of Jewish Studies,1981, Division A: The Period of the Bible*. Jerusalem: World Union of Jewish Studies, 1982.

———. "Parallelism." *EHLL*. 3:15–19.

———. "Parallelism in Hebrew and Chinese Poetry." In *Philarchisophia in the Chinese and World Perspectives*. Edited by Yang Shi. Beijin: Social Sciences Documentation Publishing House, forthcoming.

———. "Poetic Nature of the Hebrew Narrative Prose in I Samuel 2:12–17." Pages 293–304 in *Verse in Ancient Near Eastern Prose*. Edited by Johannes C. de Moor and Wilfred G. E. Watson. AOAT 42. Neukirchen-Vluyn: Neukirchener Verlag, 1993.

———. "Polysemy and Parallelism in Hab 1,8–9." *ZAW* 120 (2008): 194–203.

———. Review of *Word-Order Variation in Biblical Hebrew Poetry: Differentiating Pragmatics and Poetics*, by Nicholas P. Lunn. *BBR* 19 (2009): 599–600.

———. *The Second Book of Samuel*. NICOT. Grand Rapids: Eerdmans, 2019.

———. "The Speaker-Oriented Connective Particle *'Al-Kēn* in 2 Sam. 7:22." *JSS* 65 (2020): 85–91.

———. "Statement–Development–Twist–Denouement: The AA'XB Pattern in Biblical Hebrew Poetry." Pages 269–72 in *Prince of the Orient: A Memorial Volume for H. I. H. Prince Takahito Mikasa*. Edited by Ichiro Nakata et al. Orient Supplement 1. Tokyo: Near Eastern Studies in Japan, 2019.

———. "Vertical Grammar—The Grammar of Parallelism." Pages 55–59 in *The First Book of Samuel*. NICOT. Grand Rapids: Eerdmans, 2007.

———. "Vertical Grammar: The Grammar of Parallelism in Biblical Hebrew." Pages 487–97 in *Hamlet on a Hill: Semitic and Greek Studies Presented to Professor T. Muraoka on the Occasion of His Sixty-Fifth Birthday*. Edited by Martin F. J. Baasten and Wido Th. van Peursen. Leuven: Peeters, 2003.

———. "Vertical Grammar of Biblical Hebrew Parallelism: The AXX'B Pattern in Tetracolons." *VT* 69 (2019): 447–59.

———. "Vertical Grammar of Parallelism in Hebrew Poetry." *JBL* 128 (2009): 167–81.

———. "Vertical Grammar of Parallelism in Ugaritic Poetry." Pages 269–79 in *"Like 'Ilu Are You Wise": Studies in Northwest Semitic Languages and Literatures in Honor of Dennis G. Pardee*. Edited by H. H. Hardy II, Joseph Lam, and Eric D. Reymond. Chicago: Oriental Institute, 2022.

———. "Verticality in Biblical Hebrew Parallelism." Pages 189–206 in *Advances in Biblical Hebrew Linguistics: Data, Methods, and Analyses*. Edited by Adina Moshavi and Tania Notarius. LSAWS 12. Winona Lake, IN: Eisenbrauns, 2017.

———. "The Vetitive Particle אי and the Poetic Structure of Proverb 31:4." *AJBI* 4 (1978): 23–31.

Wagner, Andreas. "Der Parallelismus membrorum zwischen poetischer Form und Denkfigur." Pages 1–26 in *Parallelismus membrorum*. Edited by Andreas Wagner. OBO 224. Fribourg: Academic Press; Göttingen: Vandenhoeck & Ruprecht, 2007.

Watson, Wilfred G. E. *Classical Hebrew Poetry: A Guide to Its Techniques*. JSOTSSup 26. Sheffield: JSOT Press, 1984.

———. "Internal or Half-Line Parallelism in Classical Hebrew Again." *VT* 29 (1989): 44–66.

———. "Internal Parallelism in Classical Hebrew Verse." *Bib* 66 (1985): 365–84.

———. "The Pivot Pattern in Hebrew, Ugaritic, and Akkadian Poetry." *ZAW* 88 (1976): 239–53.

———. "Ugaritic Poetry." Pages 165–92 in *Handbook of Ugaritic Studies*. Edited by Wilfred G. E. Watson and Nicolas Wyatt. HdO 1.39. Leiden: Brill, 1999.

———. "Verse Patterns in the Song of Songs." *JNSL* 21 (1995): 111–22.

———. "Verse-Patterns in Ugaritic, Akkadian and Hebrew Poetry." *UF* 7 (1975): 483–92.

Wendland, Ernst R. "Aspects of the Principle of 'Parallelism' in Hebrew Poetry." *JNSL* 33 (2007): 101–24.

———. Review of *The Basics of Hebrew Poetry: Theory and Practice*, by Samuel T. S. Goh. https://tinyurl.com/SBLPress2640a.

Willis, John T. "Alternating (ABA'B') Parallelism in the Old Testament Psalms and Prophetic Literature." Pages 49–76 in *Directions in Biblical Hebrew Poetry*. Edited by Elaine R. Follis. JSOTSup 40. Sheffield: JSOT Press, 1987.

Wyatt, Nicolas. "The Darkness of Genesis I 2." *VT* 43 (1993): 543-54.

———. *Religious Texts from Ugarit: The Words of Ilimilku and His Colleagues*. Biblical Seminar 53. Sheffield: Sheffield Academic, 1998.

Zevit, Ziony. "Roman Jakobson, Psycholinguistics, and Biblical Poetry." *JBL* 109 (1990): 385–401.

Ancient Sources Index

Hebrew Bible/Old Testament		
Genesis		
1	109–10	
1:2	72, 109–10	
1:27	110	
27:39	29	
37	vii	
38	vii	
38:7	106	
49:26	94	
Exodus		
25:7	34	
34:29–35	100	
Numbers		
23:3	68	
23:15	68	
24:1	106	
Deuteronomy		
12:25	106	
32:42	34, 55, 57	
Joshua		
6:13	95	
20:8	95	
21:27	95	
1 Samuel		
2:2	31	
2:3	31	
2:10	100	
2:12	109	
2:13	31	
2:14	107	
2:17	109	
3:1	31	
5:4	76	
12:17	106, 109	
16:18	108	
17:6	109	
17:12–13	109	
18:2	109	
18:6	109	
20:13	109	
28:19	31, 105	
2 Samuel		
1:21	30–31	
1:23	18	
3:22	109	
3:33–34	38, 73–74	
7:18–29	111	
7:22	38, 111–112	
7:27	111	
12:9	31	
14:9	109	
18:33	74	
22:12	67–68	
22:15	109	
1 Kings		
22:44	62	
2 Kings		
5:12	97	
9:35	76	
12:3	61–62

2 Kings (cont.)		18:11	17, 67–68
14:4	61–62	18:14	50–51, 116
15:4	61–62	18:17	88
15:35	61–62	18:19	89
16:4	61–62	18:41	19, 53–55, 59
23:29	77	19:14	66
		22:2	23, 31
2 Chronicles		22:8	89–90
11:13	68	22:31	87
28:4	61–62	23:1	27, 33
		24:3	7
Nehemiah		24:6	22, 62–63, 108
9:31	97	25:4	15
		25:6	89
Job		29:5	44–45
1:6	68	29:9	103
2:1	68	34:9–10	79–80
5:14	4	38:3	34
5:15	60	40:7	31
5:25	60	41:4	90
6:9	60	46:6	31–32
12:24–25	38, 72–74, 78, 110	47:5	11
13:4	5	49:8	31
40:5	52	49:14	31, 103
41:20	119	49:15	87–88
		49:20	63
Psalms		51:16	31
1:6	9	51:18	31
2:2	68–69	51:21	31
2:4	22, 65–66	60:2	90
2:6	40, 59–60	79:11	4
2:8	50	86:12	31
3:4	103	89:17	100
5:7	31	89:36–37	38, 74–75, 113
6:11	31	92:7–9	27–28
8:4	49	92:9	30, 33
9:6	38–39, 70–71, 78	105:20	50–51
9:15	31	106:24–25	34
11:5	74	112:2	63
14:5	63	113:5–6	34
17:1	38, 74–78, 113	132:14	90–91
17:2	70	139:1	27, 33
18:1	27, 33	139:7	9
18:7	91	141:6	90
18:8	21, 119	146:4	119

150:6	28	30:11	97
		34:9	34
Proverbs		42:5	75
2:1	15, 40	46:28	97
2:13	15		
3:5–10	83–84	Lamentations	
3:6	14–15	5:2	12
5:15	10		
12:3	82	Ezekiel	
12:6	82	11:13	97
15:8	8	20:17	97
20:1	82		
21:24	82	Daniel	
23:15–16	32, 35	10:10	76
26:14	50		
31:4	30	Hosea	
		2:1	103
Song of Songs		9:16	29
2:12	93–94	11:2	61–2
5:1	32–33, 41, 60	11:10	38, 75, 78
5:2	41–43, 60		
5:5	75–77	Joel	
5:6	28, 77	2:3	21, 65
5:12	35–37	2:7	15
8:14	77–78	3:19	21, 65
		Amos	
Isaiah			
1:27	50	1:5	38–39, 70–72, 78, 113
2:3	15	3:7–8	80–81
8:2	75		
15:9	97	Micah	
34:6	34	2:2	12
35:4	38, 75, 78	2:4	38, 75, 78
40:16	44–45	4:2	15
45:19	110	7:3	19, 53–55, 59
60:14	76		
62:8–9	34, 55–57	Nahum	
64:10	21, 65	1:8	96–98
65:3	61–62		
		Habakkuk	
Jeremiah		1:2	12
4:23	37, 50, 52, 72, 110	1:4	70, 81
12:7	12	1:7	69–70
12:10	21, 65	1:8	39–40
14:14	5	1:9	102

Habakkuk (cont.)

1:10	96
1:13	81
1:16	61–62
2:1	60
2:4	99
2:4–5	81–83
2:8	16
2:18	5
3:3	50
3:4	98–102
3:6	61
3:8	69
3:13	38, 63–64, 75, 78
3:16	53–54, 59

Zechariah

6:5	68

New Testament

Revelation

1:7	75
3:14	75
19:11	75

Ugaritic Texts (KTU)

1. 2.i.18–19	116
1. 2.i.37–38	115
1. 2.iv.13–14	118
1. 2.iv.15–16	118–19
1. 2.iv.20–21	118
1. 2.iv.23–24	118
1. 3.i.18–19	118
1. 3.i.20–22	117–18
1. 3.iii.20–22	115–16
1. 3.iii.28–31	120–21
1. 3.iv.48–53	40
1. 3.v.40–43	40
1. 4.i.12–18	40
1. 4.iii.43–44	102
1. 4.iv.52–57	40
1. 4.vi.58–59	102
1. 5.iv.15–16	102
1.10.ii.21–22	100
1.14.i.26–27	37, 52, 116–17
1.14.i.33–35	37, 52, 116
1.14.ii.13–14	102
1.14.iii.53–54	102
1.15.iii.19	63
1.18.iv.24–26	119–20
1.18.iv.36–37	119–20
1.23.33–35	76

Modern Authors Index

Alter, Robert 37
Andersen, Francis I. 38, 100–102
Anderson, A. A. 73
Avishur, Yitsḥak 25
Baker, David W. 101
Berlin, Adele 2–4, 12, 35, 44–45
Boodberg, Peter A. 2–3, 5
Bordreuil, Pierre 116–17, 120
Brower, Robert H. 98
Canby, Jeanny Vorys 119
Cassuto, Umberto 109
Caton, Steve C. 13
Ceresko, Anthony R. 94
Chavel, Simeon 21, 34–35, 55–57
Claasen, Walter T. 79, 112
Clines, David J. A. 2, 6, 8–9, 44–46
Cohen, Alvin P. 2–3
Collins, Terence 2–3, 6–7
Collon, Dominique 101
Dahood, Mitchell 11, 25, 40, 96–97
Dobbs-Allsopp, F. W. 71, 85
Driver, Godfrey Rolles 96–97
Edelman, Diana Vikander 62
Exum, J. Cheryl 33, 36
Fox, Michael V. 76
Freedman, David Noel 38, 73
Garrett. Duane A. 36, 76
Geller, Stephen A. 2–3
Gevirtz, Stanley 96
Gordon, Cyrus H. 10, 93–94, 100–101, 118–19
Greenstein, Edward L. 2, 30
Greenberg, Moshe 111

Gzella, Holger 18
Haak, Robert D. 60, 62, 100–101
Herbert, Edward D. 74
Hess, Richard S. 36–37, 76
Hiebert, Theodore 98, 101
Jakobson, Roman 2–4, 13–14, 25–26
Kao, Yu-Kung 14
Keel, Othmar 36, 76
Keil, Carl Friedrich 96
Kselman, John S. 94, 110
Kugel, James L. 3, 6
Lambdin, Thomas O. 97
Landy, Francis 3
Liu, David Jason 8
Loewenstamm, Samuel E. 2, 30, 33
Lowth, Robert 1–2, 8, 25, 43, 45
Lunn, Nicholas P. 3, 5, 10–11, 15–17, 33, 42
Lyons, John 44
McCarter, P. Kyle, Jr. 67, 73–74, 105–8
Melamed, Ezra Z. 21, 23
Michel, Diethelm 97
Miller, Cynthia L. 12, 50, 55
Moers, Gerald 5
Muraoka, Takamitsu 24
Murphy, Roland E. 36
Niccacci, Alviero 6, 11–14
Noegel, Scott B. 94
Notarius, Tania 7
O'Connor, M. 2–3
Pardee, Dennis 2–3, 9, 13–16, 40, 45–46, 59, 115–20
Pope, Marvin H. 37, 76

Qimron, Elishaʿ	73
Rendsburg, Gary	94
Revell, E. J.	106
Roberts, J. J. M.	60–61, 98–99
Schafer, Edward H.	3
Schramm, Gene M.	93
Shupak, Nili	99–101
Smith, J. M. P.	96–97
Stager, Lawrence E.	77
Segert, Stanislav	26
Taber, Charles R.	44
Wagner, Andreas	4–5, 18
Watson, Wilfred G. E.	2–3, 7, 10, 13, 18–19, 26, 28–29, 33, 40–41, 71, 94
Wendland, Ernst R.	5, 16
Willis, John T.	34–35
Wyatt, Nicolas	110, 117
Zevit, Ziony	3

Subject Index

ABB'A', 71–75. *See also* mirror image
ABXB', 78–83. *See also* twist
Akkadian, 47, 101
alternating parallelism. *See* parallelism: alternating
antithetical parallelism. *See* parallelism: antithetical
apposition, 49–50, 121
assonance, 33, 41–42, 60, 67, 118
AX and B, vii, 74. *See also* interrupted coordination
AXB, vii, 20–22, 26, 30–31, 63, 75. *See also* literary insertion
AXX'A', 71–72. *See also* envelope construction
AXX'B, vii, 70–78. *See also* bicolon, inserted
AXYB, AxyB, 39, 74. *See also* AXX'B; bicolon, inserted
ballast variant, viii, 10–11, 39, 50, 57, 72, 78, 116
bicolon, inserted, 38–39, 70–78, 113. *See also* AXX'B
chiasm(us), 6, 9–10, 29, 63, 91, 98, 105
Chinese, 1–2, 8, 47, 78, 82
contiguity, 14, 31, 86
coreference, 11, 50, 65, 68
crux interpretatum, 63, 98, 101
deep grammar. *See* grammar: deep
discourse, vii, 80–83, 112
double segmentation, 7, 14, 85, 123
double-duty, 10–13, 48–50, 68
ellipsis, 10–12, 20, 42–43, 47–57, 115–19. *See also* gapping
end-stopping, 6, 85–86, 123

enjambment, 6, 66, 71, 85–91
envelope construction, 38–39, 71–72, 106. *See also* AXX'A'
expanded colon, 2, 25–28, 30, 33
explicative *waw*, 88, 108
gapping, 10–13, 20, 48, 50, 53, 55. *See also* ellipsis
grammar
 deep, 10, 48
 horizontal, 14, 24, 47–50, 54, 60, 64, 68, 108–109, 123. *See* grammar: vertical
 vertical, 4, 9, 12–24, et passim. *See also* grammar: horizontal
hendiadys, vii, 20, 23, 65–66, 86, 89
hinge, 103
horizontal grammar. *See* grammar: horizontal
hyponymous parallelism. *See* parallelism: hyponymous
interrupted coordination, 74. *See also* AX and B
interruption, vii, 13, 20, 26, 39, 74–75, 80–83. *See also* literary insertion, AXB, twist, ABXB'
Janus parallelism, 93–103. *See also* wordplay
Japanese, 78, 82–83, 98
linearity, 83, 123. *See also* verticality
literary insertion, vii, 20, 30, 63. *See also* AXB
merism(us), 54, 56, 60, 66
mirror image, 35, 39, 71, 73, 75. *See also* ABB'A'
monocolon, 26–29, 31–33, 39

nonparallel lines, 15, 42, 118
paradigm, 6, 13–15, 47
parallelism
    alternating, 34–35, 55, 57
    antithetical, 25, 43, 82
    hyponymous, 9, 44–46
    of greater precision, 2, 6–8, 44–45
    phonetic, 1, 15, 25–26, 33, 40–43, 59–60, 67, 118
    synonymous, 1, 8–9, 25, 43–45, 65, 75, 97
    synonymous-sequential, 19
    synthetic, 1–2, 8, 25, 43, 45
patient, 10
phonetic parallelism. *See* parallelism: phonetic
polysemy, 39, 98
rhyme, 16, 41, 59
Russian, 1–4
scansion, 6–7, 14, 33, 59, 71–74, 85–91, 102, 123
segmentation, 6–7, 14, 71, 85, 123
simple sentence, 6, 11, 17–19, 42–43, 56–70, 117–21
speaker-oriented particle, 79, 90, 111–12
superimposition, 3–10, 43
synonymous parallelism. *See* parallelism: synonymous
synonymous-sequential parallelism. *See* parallelism: synonymous-sequential
syntagm, 3–5, 13–14, 109
synthetic parallelism. *See* parallelism: synthetic
twist, 78–83. *See also* ABXB′
Ugarit, 1, 3, 25, 37, 40, 43, 47, 52, 63, 76, 96, 100, 102, 115–21
verbal ellipsis, 11–12, 42–43, 49–52, 57, 115–19
horizontal grammar. *See* grammar: horizontal
vertical grammar, 4, 9, 12–24, et passim. *See also* horizontal grammar
verticality, 14–18, 123, et passim. *See also* linearity
word order, 3, 8–10, 68, 110
word pair, 5, 15, 25, 43–44, 72–76, 96, 100, 110
wordplay, 93, 95, 103. *See also* Janus parallelism

www.ingramcontent.com/pod-product-compliance
Lightning Source LLC
Chambersburg PA
CBHW031403230426
43670CB00006B/624